Chicken Wings

Chicken Wings

70 unbeatable recipes for fried, baked and grilled wings, plus sides and drinks

Carol Hilker

photography by Toby Scott

RYLAND PETERS & SMALL

LONDON • NEW YORK

This book is dedicated to Lola and
Lennon (my cats).

Designer Maria Lee-Warren
Commissioning Editor Nathan Joyce
Production Controller
Sarah Kulasek-Boyd
Editorial Director Julia Charles
Art Director Leslie Harrington
Publisher Cindy Richards

**Stylist and Photographic Art
Direction** Luis Peral
Food Stylist Rosie Reynolds
Indexer Sandra Shotter

First published in the UK in 2015
by Ryland Peters & Small

20–21 Jockey's Fields
London WC1R 4BW and
341 E 116th St
New York
NY 10029

www.rylandpeters.com

10 9 8 7 6 5 4 3 2 1

Text © Carol Hilker 2015

Design and photographs
© Ryland Peters & Small 2015

ISBN: 978-1-84975-656-3

A CIP record for this book is available
from the British Library

US Library of Congress Cataloging-in-
Publication Data has been applied for.

Printed in China

Notes

• All spoon measurements are level
unless otherwise specified.

• Eggs used in this book are (UK) medium
and (US) large unless otherwise stated.

Contents

Introduction

Chicken wings are a weird thing. They are one of those food trends that happened, but stayed way beyond their expected timeline. Most foods that are as coveted and celebrated as the chicken wing have been around for decades, but chicken wings have their own unique tale. They just sort of appeared one day in July of 1977 in the city of Buffalo, New York.

What started as mini-fried chicken smothered in hot sauce, has now evolved into a worldwide phenomenon. Chicken wings are not just fried, but baked, smoked, grilled, double fried, slow-cooked – you name it, and it's been done (and all of these techniques are used in this book).

In the USA, chicken wings are synonymous with sports, friendship, camaraderie and the ups and downs of winning and losing. You can work up quite an appetite while watching your favourite sports team!

This book goes beyond classic chicken wings, although there are quite a selection of them in there. It also explores the way chicken wings are prepared and enjoyed in many different cultures, so I hope you'll enjoy sampling the delicious results.

Welcome to the world of chicken wings and other things!

Classics

Sweet & Spicy Wings

1.8 kg/4 lbs. chicken wings, halved at the joint, tips discarded

350 ml/1$\frac{1}{2}$ cups Louisiana-style hot sauce

175 g/$\frac{3}{4}$ cup butter

340 g/1 cup runny honey

pinch of garlic salt

1 teaspoon cayenne pepper, or to taste

salt and freshly ground black pepper

Serves 4

Honey and hot sauce – it doesn't get more Deep South than that. A little bit of sugar and a little bit of spice go a long way in this timeless dish.

Preheat the oven to 180°C (350°F) Gas 4. Grease the base of a large casserole or roasting dish.

Place the chicken in the dish and sprinkle with salt and pepper. Bake, uncovered, for 50–60 minutes in the preheated oven, turning the chicken over halfway through.

Combine the hot sauce, butter, honey, garlic salt, cayenne pepper and a pinch of freshly ground black pepper in a medium saucepan. Place over a low-medium heat and melt the butter, stirring well. Increase the heat to medium-high and bring to the boil, continuing to stir, then reduce the heat to low-medium and cook for 40–45 minutes, stirring occasionally. The sauce will thicken to a syrupy consistency and will reduce by half.

When the chicken is cooked and the juices run clear when the thickest part is pierced to the bone, remove from the oven and drain off any cooking juices. Pour half the sauce into the dish and toss the chicken. Return to the oven for 5 minutes (or place under a preheated grill/ broiler). To serve, pour the remaining sauce over.

Serve with Blue Cheese Dipping Sauce (see page 29).

Buttermilk-crumbed Wings

The best fried chicken always involves buttermilk, with the tangy marinade making it one of the juiciest and tastiest ways to cook chicken. This recipe is a classic.

3 eggs

500 ml/2 cups buttermilk

1.8 kg/4 lbs. chicken wings, halved at the joints, tips removed

400 g/3 cups plain/all-purpose flour

60 g/1 cup crushed saltine crackers or cornflakes

1 teaspoon freshly ground black pepper

1 teaspoon dried thyme

1/4 teaspoon cayenne pepper

1 teaspoon salt, plus extra for seasoning

1/2 teaspoon garlic powder

vegetable oil, for frying

Dijon-Blue Cheese Dipping Sauce:

100 ml/1/2 cup mayonnaise

120 ml/1/2 cup sour cream

2 teaspoons freshly squeezed lemon juice

2 teaspoons red wine vinegar

1 teaspoon creamy Dijon mustard

1/4 teaspoon Worcestershire sauce

50 g/1/3 cup crumbled blue cheese

1 garlic clove, finely chopped

1-2 tablespoons chopped fresh flat-leaf parsley

1 spring onion/scallion, finely chopped

salt and freshly ground black pepper

Serves 4

Beat the eggs and buttermilk together in a large bowl until smooth. Mix in the chicken wings, cover, and refrigerate for 30 minutes.

Preheat the oven to 220°C (425°F) Gas 7. Line 2–3 large baking sheets with foil.

Combine the flour and crackers/cornflakes with the pepper, thyme, cayenne pepper, salt and garlic powder in a large bowl.

Remove the chicken wings from the buttermilk marinade and discard the remaining marinade. Allow the excess buttermilk to drip from the wings, then press into the crumbs to coat.

Arrange the chicken wings on the baking sheets. Bake in the preheated oven for 25–35 minutes or until golden brown and the juices run clear when the thickest part is pierced to the bone. Remove from the oven.

Preheat the oil in a deep fryer set to 190°C (375°F). Fry the wings in batches for a few minutes to crisp them. Drain on a plate lined with paper towels and season to taste with salt. Serve with Dijon-Blue Cheese Dipping Sauce (see below).

Dijon-Blue Cheese Dipping Sauce

Stir or whisk the mayonnaise, sour cream, lemon juice, vinegar, mustard and Worcestershire sauce in a bowl until smooth. Add the blue cheese, garlic, parsley and spring onion/scallion, and stir until combined. Season to taste, then cover and refrigerate for at least 1 hour before serving.

Baked Bourbon Wings

120 ml/$\frac{1}{2}$ cup soy sauce

60 ml/$\frac{1}{4}$ cup vegetable oil

60 ml/$\frac{1}{4}$ cup cider vinegar

60 ml/$\frac{1}{4}$ cup bourbon

50 g/$\frac{1}{4}$ cup brown sugar

1 teaspoon ground ginger

1 tablespoon finely chopped garlic

$\frac{1}{2}$ a large onion, diced

1.8 kg/4 lbs. chicken wings, halved at the joints, tips removed

Chipotle-Ranch Sauce:

225 g/1 cup light mayonnaise

250 ml/1 cup sour cream

3 tablespoons Ranch Seasoning (see page 49)

3 spring onions/scallions, finely chopped

1 garlic clove, finely chopped

1 canned chipotle chilli/chile, finely chopped

1 tablespoon freshly squeezed lime juice

Serves 4–6

This is a sweet and smoky sauce that slightly resembles a BBQ sauce, but has a base of cooked-down bourbon as its main star. The recipe gets its name not only from the use of bourbon, but also because the dish originated on Bourbon Street in Memphis, Tennessee.

Combine the soy sauce, oil, vinegar, bourbon, brown sugar, ginger, garlic and diced onion in a bowl. Whisk until combined.

Place the chicken in a large baking dish and pour the sauce over. Toss to coat each piece of chicken with sauce. Cover the dish and marinate in the refrigerator overnight (or for at least 4 hours).

Preheat the oven to 180°C (350°F) Gas 4.

Uncover the chicken and bake for 45 minutes in the preheated oven. Turn the pieces several times during cooking to ensure they bake in the sauce on both sides.

When the chicken is cooked through and the juices run clear when the thickest part is pierced to the bone, remove from the oven. Preheat a grill/broiler to a moderate heat and place the baking dish underneath. Cook for 5–10 minutes to brown the chicken.

Serve immediately, with any extra sauce poured over. These wings are great served with Chipotle Ranch Sauce (see below) and rice.

Chipotle-Ranch Sauce

Place all the ingredients in a bowl and whisk until thoroughly combined.

Smoked Chipotle Wings

3 large handfuls hickory wood chips, divided

1.8 kg/4 lbs. chicken wings, halved at the joints, tips removed

6 tablespoons Cajun seasoning, or as needed

3 tablespoons butter

3 tablespoons finely chopped garlic

1 litre/4 cups hot sauce (such as Frank's Red Hot ®)

vegetable oil, for frying

Chipotle-Sour Cream Dip:

210-g/7-oz. can of chipotle chillies/chiles in adobo sauce

450 ml/2 cups sour cream

1 tablespoon ground cumin

freshly squeezed juice of 1 lime

salt

Serves 4–6

This recipe uses a smoker with hickory wood chips, creating a rich, smokey flavour. The wings are then fried and grilled, giving them a wonderfully crispy texture. The extra effort is definitely worth it.

Preheat the smoker to 95°C (200°F) and add 1 handful of wood chips to start the smoke rolling.

Liberally coat the chicken wings with half of the Cajun seasoning.

Place the wings directly on the grate in the smoker or in an aluminium pan with holes to allow airflow. Smoke the wings for 2 hours, adding more wood chips as necessary.

Combine the butter, garlic and remaining Cajun seasoning in a large saucepan over a medium heat. Cook the mixture for about 1 minute, stirring, until the butter has melted. Stir the hot sauce into the butter mixture and lower the heat, simmering the mixture for about 30 minutes, stirring occasionally, until the sauce has thickened.

Preheat the oil in a deep fryer set to 190°C (375°F). Preheat a grill/broiler to 190°C (375°F).

Remove the wings from the smoker and cook, 10–12 at a time, in the deep fryer for 5–7 minutes, until they are cooked through and are lightly browned on the outside.

Transfer the cooked wings to a baking sheet and liberally coat each wing with hot sauce mixture. Place the coated wings directly onto the wire rack of the preheated grill/broiler and cook for 2–3 minutes on each side, until the sauce has caramelized and the wings are crisp. Serve with Chipotle-Sour Cream Wing Dip (see below).

Chipotle-Sour Cream Dip

Place the chillies/chiles in a blender with the sour cream, cumin, lime juice and a few good pinches of salt. Pulse in the blender until well combined. Refrigerate for at least 2 hours before serving.

Not Your Dad's BBQ Wings

1.8 kg/4 lbs. chicken wings, halved at the joints, tips removed

1 small onion, finely chopped

250 ml/1 cup teriyaki sauce

250 ml/1 cup oyster sauce

120 ml/^{1}/$_2$ cup soy sauce

140 ml/^{1}/$_2$ cup Homemade Ketchup (see page 74)

4 tablespoons garlic powder

120 ml/^{1}/$_2$ cup gin

2 teaspoons cayenne pepper

1 teaspoon dry mustard

200 g/1 cup brown sugar

80 g/^{1}/$_2$ cup runny honey

Serves 4

The wings are both a little bit old school and a little bit new school! The ketchup, garlic, mustard and cayenne are pretty standard ingredients, but the addition of teriyaki and oyster and soy sauces brings an Asian twist to this otherwise classic American dish.

In a large bowl, mix the onion, teriyaki sauce, oyster sauce, soy sauce, ketchup, garlic powder, gin, cayenne pepper, dry mustard and brown sugar. Place the chicken wings in the bowl, cover, and marinate in the refrigerator for 8 hours or overnight.

Preheat the grill/broiler to low.

Lightly oil the wire rack of the grill/broiler. Arrange the chicken under the grill/broiler, discarding the marinade. Grill/broil the chicken wings on one side for 20 minutes, then turn and brush with honey. Continue grilling/broiling for 25 minutes, or until cooked through and the juices run clear when the thickest part is pierced to the bone.

These wings are good served with Blue Cheese Dipping Sauce (see page 29).

Bacon & Cheddar Wings

1.8 kg/4 lbs. chicken wings, halved at the joints, tips removed

1/4 teaspoon freshly ground black pepper

12 streaky/American bacon rashers/slices, cut in half crosswise

Cheese Sauce:

500 ml/2 cups whole milk

60 g/1/4 cup unsalted butter, cut into pieces

35 g/1/4 cup plain/all-purpose flour

200 g/2 cups mature Cheddar cheese, grated

2 tablespoons hot sauce, such as Tabasco (optional)

1 teaspoon cayenne pepper (optional)

salt and freshly ground black pepper

Serves 4–6

With the addition of bacon, this might seem like meat overload, but it's really very delicious. Don't be tempted to omit the melted Cheddar sauce – once you try this recipe, you'll understand!

Preheat the oven to 220°C (425°F) Gas 7. Line two baking sheets with foil and grease with cooking spray.

Sprinkle the chicken with black pepper. Wrap each chicken piece with half a rasher/slice of bacon and place on the baking sheets. Set aside while you make the sauce.

Heat the milk in a medium saucepan over a low-medium heat. When it starts to bubble, remove from the heat and set aside.

Put the butter in a separate, medium saucepan and melt gently over a medium heat. Sprinkle the flour on top and whisk for 1–2 minutes until a thick paste forms. Remove the pan from the heat. Slowly add the warm milk to the butter/flour mixture in a steady stream, whisking until well blended. Return the pan to a medium-high heat and bring to a boil, stirring continuously until thickened. Remove the pan from the heat, add the cheese, and whisk until smooth. Stir in the hot sauce (if using), cayenne pepper (if using), and salt and pepper to taste.

Cover the pan to prevent a skin forming on the sauce and set aside. The sauce will thicken upon cooling.

Place the chicken in the preheated oven and bake for 30 minutes, then turn the chicken over and rotate the baking sheets in the oven. Bake for a further 20–30 minutes or until golden brown and the juices run clear when the thickest part is pierced to the bone.

Toss the wings in half the cheese sauce, reserving the remaining sauce for dipping.

Sweet & Sour
with Bacon Wings

1.8 kg/4 lbs. chicken wings, halved at the joints, tips removed

450 g/1 lb. smoked streaky/American bacon rashers/slices

130 g/1 cup plain/all-purpose flour

1 teaspoon salt

1 teaspoon freshly ground black pepper

vegetable oil, for frying

cocktail sticks/toothpicks

Sweet & Sour Sauce:

150 g/^{3}/$_4$ cup white sugar

75 ml/^{1}/$_3$ cup white wine vinegar

60 ml/^{1}/$_4$ cup soy sauce

1 tablespoon Homemade Ketchup (see page 74)

2 tablespoons cornflour/cornstarch

150 ml/^{2}/$_3$ cup water

125 g/^{1}/$_2$ cup chopped pineapple

Serves 4-6

These chicken wings are a fantastic play on the Chinese take-out favourite sweet and sour chicken. The wings are fried and crispy, and the salt of the bacon mixes well with the sauce. Serve with white rice for a quick, no-wait, take-out inspired dinner.

Wrap each chicken wing in a bacon slice, securing it in place with a cocktail stick/toothpick.

Preheat the oil in a deep fryer set to 190°C (375°F).

Mix the flour, salt and pepper in a medium bowl and dip each bacon-wrapped wing. Coat well in the flour mixture, then shake off the excess.

Fry 3–4 wings at a time until they are a deep golden brown and the juices run clear when the thickest part is pierced to the bone. Remove the cocktail sticks/toothpicks.

To make the sauce, combine the sugar, vinegar, soy sauce and ketchup in a medium saucepan. In a bowl, blend the cornflour/cornstarch with 2 tablespoons of the water and mix together until smooth. Stir in the remaining water and pineapple, then pour the mixture into the saucepan. Bring to a boil, stirring well, then reduce the heat and simmer until the sauce has thickened.

Pour half the sauce over the cooked wings and serve the remainder as a dipping sauce.

Bing Cherry BBQ Wings

130 g/1 cup plain/
all-purpose flour

1 teaspoon salt

1 teaspoon ground black
pepper

1.8 kg/4 lbs. chicken wings,
halved at the joints, tips
removed

vegetable oil, for frying

Cherry BBQ Sauce:

2 tablespoons butter

1 onion, chopped

3 garlic cloves, finely
chopped

400 g/2 cups fresh or
frozen Bing cherries
(or other dark, sweet
cherries), stoned/pitted
and coarsely chopped

250 g/1 cup Homemade
Ketchup (see page 74)

130 g/²/₃ cup packed brown
sugar

60 ml/¹/₄ cup cider vinegar

1 tablespoon Worcestershire
sauce

2 teaspoons mustard
powder

¹/₂ teaspoon freshly ground
black pepper

Serves 4-6

Bing cherries are deep red in colour and sweet, and their addition to this BBQ sauce turns it into something absolutely delicious. The chicken wings are fried and slathered with the sauce, but be warned – this sauce is addictive, and also makes a great accompaniment to ribs and hamburgers.

To make the sauce, melt the butter in a large saucepan, add the onion, and sauté until tender. Add the garlic and continue to cook for 1 minute. Stir in the remaining sauce ingredients. Cook, uncovered, over a medium-low heat for 20 minutes or until the cherries are tender and the sauce has thickened, stirring occasionally. Set aside and let cool.

Preheat the oil in a deep fryer set to 190°C (375°F).

Mix the flour, salt and pepper in a medium bowl and dip each wing. Coat well in the flour mixture, then shake off the excess.

Fry 3–4 wings at a time until they are a deep golden brown and the juices run clear when the thickest part is pierced to the bone. Toss the wings with half the sauce and serve the remainder as a dipping sauce.

These wings are also great served with Ranch Dipping Sauce (see page 49).

Hot & Spicy

Red Hot Buffalo Wings

canola or peanut oil, for frying

1.8 kg/4 lbs. chicken wings, halved at the joints, tips removed

170 g/1 stick plus 4 tablespoons butter

250 ml/1 cup hot sauce, such as Frank's Red Hot Original Cayenne Pepper Sauce®

celery and carrot sticks, to serve

Blue Cheese Dipping Sauce:

150 g/1 cup crumbled blue cheese

150 g/³/4 cup mayonnaise

120 ml/¹/2 cup sour cream

Serves 4–6

Frank's Red Hot Buffalo Sauce was the 'secret' ingredient used to create the original Buffalo-style wings in Buffalo, New York. It's essentially hot sauce made with cayenne pepper. This recipe has a hot base, but the use of butter gives it a slightly milder flavour.

Preheat the oven to 100°C (200°F) Gas ¼.

Preheat the oil in a deep fryer set to 180°C (350°F).

Dry the wings thoroughly with paper towels. Working in batches, fry the wings for about 12 minutes until golden brown and the juices run clear when the thickest part is pierced to the bone. Transfer the cooked wings to a wire rack set over a baking sheet, and place in the oven to keep warm until all wings are fried.

Heat the butter in a 30-cm/12-in. deep-sided frying pan/skillet over a medium heat. Stir in the hot sauce until smooth, then add the wings, and toss until completely coated. Serve the wings in a large bowl with Blue Cheese Dipping Sauce and celery and carrot sticks on the side.

Blue Cheese Dipping Sauce

Place all the ingredients in a medium bowl and whisk until combined.

Spicy Garlic & Ginger Wings

1.8 kg/4 lbs. chicken wings, halved at the joints, tips removed

salt and freshly ground black pepper

3 tablespoons hot sauce, such as Frank's Red Hot Sauce®

2 tablespoons vegetable oil

130 g/1 cup plain/ all-purpose flour

3 garlic cloves, crushed

2 tablespoons finely chopped fresh ginger root

1 tablespoon Asian chilli pepper sauce

120 ml/$\frac{1}{2}$ cup rice vinegar

100 g/$\frac{1}{2}$ cup packed brown sugar

1 tablespoon soy sauce

Parmesan-Cream Dipping Sauce:

225 g/1 cup light mayonnaise

50 g/6 tablespoons grated Parmesan cheese

4 teaspoons Dijon mustard

4 teaspoons Worcestershire sauce

Serves 4–6

These wings are flavoured with a tasty combination of garlic and ginger. They're crispy, flavourful and are a great mix with almost any dipping sauce.

Preheat the oven to 200°C (400°F) Gas 6. Line two or three baking sheets with foil and grease with cooking spray or vegetable oil.

Place the chicken in a large mixing bowl. Season with salt and pepper Add the hot sauce and the vegetable oil, and toss to coat.

Place the flour and wings in a large, resealable plastic bag. Hold the bag closed tightly, and shake to coat the wings entirely with the flour; no uncovered spots should remain. Arrange the wings on the prepared baking sheets, making sure they are not touching one another. Spray the wings with additional cooking spray or drizzle with a little more vegetable oil.

Bake in the preheated oven for 30 minutes, turn all the wings, and return to the oven to cook until crispy and the juices run clear when the thickest part is pierced to the bone.

Whisk together the garlic, ginger, chilli sauce, rice vinegar, brown sugar and soy sauce in a saucepan. Bring the mixture to a boil and immediately remove from heat.

Put roughly half the wings in a large mixing bowl. Pour about half the sauce over the wings. Toss the wings with tongs to coat evenly; transfer to a tray and let rest for about 5 minutes to allow the sauce to soak into the wings before serving. Repeat with the remaining wings and sauce. Serve with Parmesan Cream Dipping Sauce.

Parmesan-Cream Dipping Sauce

Place all the ingredients in a medium bowl and whisk until combined.

Pineapple-Habanero Wings

125 g/¹/₂ cup crushed
pineapple

120 ml/¹/₂ cup sour cream

2 tablespoons habanero
sauce, or other hot sauce

¹/₄ teaspoon salt

vegetable oil, for frying

1.8 kg/4 lbs. chicken wings,
halved at the joints, tips
removed

70 g/¹/₂ cup plain/
all-purpose flour

Pineapple Dipping
Sauce:

225 g/1 cup plain yogurt

125 g/¹/₂ cup crushed
pineapple

2 tablespoons icing/
confectioners' sugar

25 g/¹/₄ cup shredded
coconut

2 tablespoons coconut milk

Serves 4–6

This recipe is a sweeter version of hot wings. However, just because it contains pineapple doesn't mean this is a dish mild on the heat. This chicken wing recipe will definitely make you sweat!

Combine the crushed pineapple, sour cream, habanero sauce (or other hot sauce) and salt in a medium saucepan; whisk until smooth. Place over a low-medium heat and heat until warm.

Preheat the oil in a deep fryer set to 180°C (350°F).

Coat the chicken wings with flour by dredging them or tossing them in a bowl. Fry a few wings at a time for 10 minutes or until golden and crispy and the juices run clear when the thickest part is pierced to the bone. Toss the wings with warm pineapple-habanero sauce. Serve with Pineapple Dipping Sauce.

Pineapple Dipping Sauce

Combine all the ingredients in a serving bowl and refrigerate until ready to serve.

Raspberry-Jalapeño Wings

290 g/1 cup seedless raspberry jam/jelly

1½ tablespoons runny honey

2 fresh jalapeños, deseeded (unless you want them really hot) and diced

60 g/4 tablespoons butter

1 tablespoon Worcestershire sauce

1.8 kg/4 lbs. chicken wings, halved at the joints, tips removed

vegetable oil, for frying

Jalapeño–Ranch Dipping Sauce:

300 g/1¹⁄₃ cups mayonnaise

90 ml/¹⁄₃ cup buttermilk

90 ml/¹⁄₃ cup Salsa Verde (see page 132)

3 tablespoons chopped canned green chillies/chiles

2 jalapeño peppers, halved and deseeded

3 tablespoons Ranch Seasoning (see page 49)

Serves 4–6

This wing recipe is perfect for summertime BBQs. These wings are fried and then tossed in a jalapeño-raspberry salsa-like sauce. They are sweet, but also very hot, and are best served with Jalapeño-Ranch Dipping Sauce.

Combine the raspberry jam/jelly, honey and jalapeños in a small saucepan over a medium heat. Let the mixture slowly reduce to a sauce consistency, then either remove from the heat or keep warm over a very, very low heat.

Place the butter and Worcestershire sauce in a large saucepan over a medium-high heat. Once the butter has melted, add half the chicken to the pan and toss to coat. Sauté for about 5 minutes. Remove from the heat and place in a large bowl. Repeat with the remaining wings.

Preheat the oven to 200°C (400°F) Gas 6. Grease a large baking sheet with cooking spray or vegetable oil.

Preheat the oil in a deep fryer set to 180°C (350°F).

Fry 3–4 wings at a time in the oil until golden and crispy and the juices run clear when the thickest part is pierced to the bone.

After all the wings are fried, place them in a large bowl. Pour the raspberry-jalapeño mixture over the wings and toss to coat.

Transfer the coated wings to the prepared baking sheet and bake in the preheated oven for 5–10 minutes, until the sauce is sticky and the wings are warm to touch. Serve with Jalapeño-Ranch Dipping Sauce.

Jalapeño-Ranch Dipping Sauce

Place all the ingredients into a blender and process until smooth. Chill before serving.

Damn Hot Wings

vegetable oil or canola oil, for frying

1.8 kg/4 lbs. chicken wings, halved at the joints, tips removed

115 g/1 stick butter

750 ml/3 cups hot sauce

2 tablespoons chopped fresh garlic

3 jalapeño peppers, deseeded and chopped

2 Thai chilli/chile peppers, deseeded and chopped

3 habanero peppers, deseeded and chopped

2 yellow wax peppers, deseeded and chopped

3 red chilli/chile peppers, deseeded and chopped

salt and freshly ground black pepper

Serves 4–6

These are the hottest chicken wings in the whole book. A variety of hot peppers are used, along with a spicy hot sauce. Make sure you have lots of milk and water on hand to kill the burn. These are not for the faint of heart!

Preheat the oil in a deep fryer set to 180°C (350°F).

Preheat the oven to 200°C (400°F) Gas 6.

Fry the wings, 3–4 at a time, turning occasionally, until golden brown. Transfer to a shallow baking dish and bake in the preheated oven for 15 minutes, turning once, or until the juices run clear when the thickest part is pierced to the bone.

Melt the butter in a medium saucepan over a medium heat. Stir in the hot sauce, garlic and peppers. Reduce the heat to medium-low and cook for 15 minutes, or until the peppers have softened. Season to taste with salt and pepper, then pour the sauce over the wings, turning to coat.

Reduce the oven temperature to 180°C (350°F) Gas 4, return the wings to the oven and bake for a further 10 minutes.

These wings are great served with Blue Cheese Dipping Sauce (see page 29).

Brown Butter & Roasted Red Pepper Wings

1.8 kg/4 lbs. chicken wings, halved at the joints, tips removed

85 g/6 tablespoons butter

85 g/⅓ cup roasted red (bell) pepper, chopped

1½ tablespoons brown sugar

1½ tablespoons garlic powder

1½ tablespoons chilli powder

1½ tablespoons smoked paprika

2 teaspoons onion powder

kosher/flaked salt and freshly ground black pepper

Roasted Red Pepper-Paprika Cream Sauce:

85 g/⅓ cup roasted red (bell) pepper, chopped

60 g/¼ cup goat's cheese

2 tablespoons sour cream

1 tablespoon paprika

¼ teaspoon salt

Serves 4–6

The addition of spicy roasted red pepper creates deliciously savoury and slightly sweet chicken wings. They are spiced, baked and served with a Red Pepper-Paprika dipping sauce.

Preheat the oven to 220°C (425°F) Gas 7.

Line 2–3 baking sheets with foil.

Melt the butter in a large, deep saucepan over a medium-high heat until the butter browns but does not burn. Reduce the heat to low-medium and add the red (bell) pepper, brown sugar, garlic powder, chilli powder, paprika and onion powder. Season to taste with kosher/flaked salt and ground black pepper and mix well.

Remove the pan from the heat. Add half the chicken wings to the pan, stir to coat with the butter mixture, then leave to infuse for about 5 minutes. Transfer the infused wings to a prepared baking sheet, then infuse the remaining wings and add them to another prepared baking sheet.

Bake in the preheated oven for 25 minutes, turning them halfway through, until the juices run clear when the thickest part is pierced to the bone. Serve immediately with the dipping sauce below.

Roasted Red Pepper-Paprika Cream Sauce

Mix all the ingredients in a blender until thoroughly combined and smooth. Refrigerate until ready to serve.

Harissa-Honey Hot Wings

1.8 kg/4 lbs. chicken wings, halved at the joints, tips removed

90 g/6 tablespoons harissa

1 tablespoon runny honey

Serves 4–6

This sweet and spicy combo uses harissa and honey for an unforgettable flavour. Baking, followed by grilling/broiling makes for perfect, fall-off-the-bone wings with wonderfully crispy skin.

Preheat the oven to 190°C (375°F) Gas 5.

Line 2–3 baking sheets with foil.

Line up the wings on the baking sheets and bake for 30 minutes, until almost cooked through.

While the wings are baking, preheat the grill/broiler to high. When wings have finished in the oven, grill/broil them for 3–5 minutes, until the skin is crispy and the juices run clear when the thickest part is pierced to the bone.

Mix the harissa and honey together in a large bowl. Transfer the cooked wings to the bowl and stir to coat. The harissa mixture is thick, but the heat of the wings will soften it.

These wings are fantastic served with Honey-Sriracha Sauce (see page 50).

Yuzu Pao

2 tablespoons coriander
seeds

$^1/_2$ teaspoon cumin seeds

$^1/_2$ teaspoon ground
cinnamon

$^1/_2$ tablespoon salt

2 tablespoons olive oil

1.8 kg/4 lbs. chicken wings,
halved at the joints, tips
removed

120 g/$^1/_2$ cup red yuzu pao
sauce (or sriracha sauce
mixed with 1 teaspoon
yuzu juice or lemon juice)

3 tablespoons runny honey

3 tablespoons chopped,
fresh flat-leaf parsley

mangetout/sugar snap
peas, to serve

Serves 4–6

This Japanese spice mixture is hot and spicy, but it's a different kind of heat than the average Buffalo hot wing heat; it's a body-cleansing kind of heat – fragrant and delicious. But be warned – this dish that will make your upper lip sweat and your eyes a little brighter!

Toast the coriander and cumin seeds and the cinnamon in a small, dry pan over a medium heat until fragrant, then let cool. Use a coffee grinder, spice grinder or pestle and mortar to grind the cooled spices to a fine powder.

Combine the spices, salt, and olive oil in a large bowl. Add the wings and stir to coat, then cover and marinate in the refrigerator overnight or for at least 4 hours.

Preheat the oven to 190°C (375°F) Gas 5.

Spread the marinated wings on 2–3 baking sheets. Bake in the preheated oven for 50 minutes or until the wings are golden and the juices run clear when the thickest part is pierced to the bone. Set aside to cool slightly.

Combine the red yuzu pao sauce and the honey in a small bowl. Place the cooked wings in a large bowl, add the yuzu pao-honey mixture and half the parsley, then toss to coat. Serve hot, garnished with the remaining parsley and with mangetout/sugar snap peas on the side.

Spicy Grilled Orange-Honey Mustard Wings

1.8 kg/4 lbs. chicken wings, halved at the joints, tips removed

125 g/^{1}/$_2$ cup Dijon mustard

60 g/^{1}/$_4$ cup, plus 1 tablespoon runny honey

3 tablespoons mayonnaise

2 teaspoons steak sauce or Worcestershire sauce

zest of 1 orange

coleslaw and mini corn on the cobs, to serve

Serves 4–6

The Dijon mustard gives these wings a tangy kick, but the key ingredient is the steak sauce. This recipe is simple, delicious and proof that you don't need a lot of bells and whistles to make good food.

Preheat the grill/broiler to medium.

Mix the mustard, honey, mayonnaise, orange zest and steak sauce together in a small bowl. Set aside a small amount of the honey-mustard sauce for basting, and dip the chicken into the remaining sauce to coat.

Lightly oil the grill rack. Grill the chicken for 20–25 minutes, turning occasionally, or until the chicken is cooked through and the juices run clear when the thickest part is pierced to the bone. Baste occasionally with the reserved sauce during the last 10 minutes.

Serve with coleslaw and mini corn on the cob.

Taco Wings

1 sachet taco seasoning mix

3 tablespoons canola oil

2 tablespoons red wine vinegar

1 teaspoon hot pepper sauce

1.8 kg/4 lbs. chicken wings, halved at the joints, tips removed

vegetable oil, for frying (optional)

Ranch Dipping Sauce:

75 g/$\frac{1}{3}$ cup mayonnaise or Greek yogurt

75 ml/$\frac{1}{3}$ cup milk

1 tablespoon ranch seasoning (see below)

1 teaspoon hot sauce (optional)

Ranch Seasoning (see note):

35 g/$\frac{1}{3}$ cup dried buttermilk or powdered milk

2 tablespoons dried parsley

1$\frac{1}{2}$ teaspoons dried dill

2 teaspoons garlic powder

2 teaspoons onion powder

2 teaspoons dried onion flakes

1 teaspoon freshly ground black pepper

1 teaspoon dried chives

1 teaspoon salt

Serves 4–6

The rich, spicy Mexican taste of these wings comes from a combination of taco seasoning, red wine vinegar and hot pepper sauce. Enjoy with a ranch dressing dip, or debone the chicken and make tacos.

Preheat the grill/broiler to medium, or heat up a barbecue.

Combine the taco seasoning, oil, vinegar and hot pepper sauce in a large resealable plastic bag. Add the chicken, seal the bag and shake to coat.

Grill/broil the chicken, turning occasionally, for 15–20 minutes or until crisp and golden and the juices run clear when the thickest part is pierced to the bone. Alternatively, preheat the oil in a deep fryer set to 180°C (350°F) and fry the chicken in batches.

Serve with the Ranch Dipping Sauce (see below), Guacamole (see page 132) and tortilla chips.

Ranch Dipping Sauce

Place the mayonnaise or yogurt, milk and ranch seasoning in a small bowl and whisk to combine. Add the hot sauce for a Hot Pepper Ranch Dipping Sauce.

Note

3 tablespoons of this ranch seasoning is the equivalent of 1 packet of store-bought seasoning mix. Any unused seasoning can be stored in an airtight container.

Honey-Sriracha Wings

vegetable or peanut oil, for frying

1.8 kg/4 lbs. chicken wings, halved at the joints, tips removed

225 g/1 cup unsalted butter, cut into 2.5-cm/1-in. pieces

180 g/^{3}/$_4$ cup sriracha sauce

165 g/^{1}/$_2$ cup runny honey

1 teaspoon freshly ground black pepper

2 teaspoons kosher/flaked salt

dash of freshly squeezed lime juice

chopped fresh flat-leaf parsley

Serves 4–6

Fried with a honey and sriracha coating, these wings are sweet and spicy, with the flavours playing off each other. The combination mixes east and west, with a little bit of the American South thrown in for good measure.

Preheat the oven to 110°C (200°F) Gas ¼.

Preheat the oil in a deep fryer to 180°C (350°F).

Fry the wings in batches for 10–12 minutes, until crispy and golden brown and the juices run clear when the thickest part is pierced to the bone. Remove from the oil and place on 2–3 baking sheets in the preheated oven to keep warm.

While the wings are frying, melt the butter in a medium saucepan over a low heat. Add the sriracha, honey, pepper, salt and lime juice, stirring to combine. Keep warm over a low heat. When the sauce is combined, remove the wings from the oven.

Put the cooked wings in a large mixing bowl and toss with the honey-sriracha sauce. Garnish with parsley and serve with Coconut Biscuits (see page 136).

If you wish to make an accompanying Sriracha-Ranch Dipping Sauce, add 1 tablespoon of sriracha to the Ranch Dipping Sauce (see page 49).

Baked Mojito Wasabi Wings

These chicken wings are an East-meets-West fusion. A mixture of a classic Mojito mint flavour and wasabi produces a hot-meets-cool taste.

1.8 kg/4 lbs. chicken wings, halved at the joints, tips removed

1 teaspoon salt

1 teaspoon freshly ground black pepper

35 g/^{1}/4 cup cornflour/ cornstarch

150 ml/^{2}/3 cup ponzu sauce

2 tablespoons runny honey

60 ml/^{1}/4 cup white rum

1 teaspoon red chilli sauce, such as sriracha

2 teaspoons garlic powder

3 tablespoons sesame seeds

vegetable oil, for frying

Mint-Wasabi Dipping Sauce:

175 ml/^{3}/4 cup Greek yogurt

^{1}/4 teaspoon wasabi powder

2 tablespoons finely chopped coriander/ cilantro

1 tablespoon freshly squeezed lime juice

2 fresh mint leaves, finely chopped

Serves 4–6

Sprinkle the chicken on all sides with salt and pepper. Dust lightly with cornflour/cornstarch and rub to coat.

Combine the ponzu, honey, rum, chilli sauce, garlic powder and 2 tablespoons of the sesame seeds in a large bowl, stirring well. Add the chicken wings and toss to coat. Cover the bowl with clingfilm/plastic wrap and place in the refrigerator for 10 minutes.

Remove the wings from the marinade, allowing the excess to dip back into the bowl. Set the wings aside.

Pour the remaining marinade into a small saucepan. Cook over a medium-high heat for 8–10 minutes, stirring frequently, and reduce until thickened and syrupy.

Preheat the oil in a deep fryer set to 180°C (350°F).

Preheat the oven to 220°C (425°F) Gas 7. Line 2–3 baking sheets with foil.

Fry the wings in batches for about 10 minutes per batch, until the coating is golden brown and the juices run clear when the thickest part is pierced to the bone.

Arrange the fried chicken wings on the baking sheets. Brush the wings with the thickened marinade, turn them over, and brush with marinade on the other side. Bake in the preheated oven for 10 minutes, then baste again with marinade and cook for a further 5 minutes. Remove from the oven and sprinkle with the remaining sesame seeds.

Mint-Wasabi Dipping Sauce

Combine all the ingredients in a small bowl and chill before serving.

Trendy 53

Double Baked Wings

1.8 kg/4 lbs. chicken wings, halved at the joints, tips removed

1 tablespoon garlic powder

1 tablespoon onion powder

1 teaspoon freshly ground black pepper

1^1/$_2$ teaspoons paprika

^{1}/$_4$ teaspoon cayenne pepper

40 g/3 tablespoons butter

350 ml/1^1/$_2$ cups hot sauce or Tabasco sauce

250 g/1 cup Homemade Ketchup (see page 74)

120 ml/^{1}/$_2$ cup Ranch Seasoning (see page 49)

120 ml/^{1}/$_2$ cup soy sauce

Serves 4–6

These crispy wings are baked until almost cooked, then coated with a Buffalo sauce and baked again. If you wish, serve them with Ranch Dipping Sauce (see pages 44) or Blue Cheese Dipping Sauce (see page 29), along with carrot and celery sticks.

Preheat the oven to 200°C (400°F) Gas 6. Line 1–2 baking sheets with foil and grease lightly with cooking spray or vegetable oil.

In a large bowl, combine the garlic, onion powder, pepper, paprika and cayenne pepper. Add the wings and toss in the spice mixture.

Arrange the wings in a single layer on the lined baking sheets. Bake the wings in the preheated oven for about 30 minutes. The skin will begin to turn brown and the meat will begin to loosen from the bone.

While the wings are baking, melt the butter in a medium saucepan over a low heat. Stir in the hot sauce (or Tabasco), ketchup, ranch seasoning and soy sauce. When the wings are done, place them in a large bowl and pour three-quarters of the sauce over them. Toss until covered.

Replace the foil on the baking sheets and rearrange the coated wings back on the sheets.

Bake the wings for a further 5–10 minutes, until the juices run clear when the thickest part is pierced to the bone. You'll have to keep an eye on them now because you will not want to overcook them. Serve with the remaining sauce drizzled over the top.

Cola Wings

1.8 kg/4 lbs. chicken wings, halved at the joints, tips removed

450 g/2 cups brown sugar (light or dark)

2 x 330-ml/11-fl. oz. cans of cola or root beer

3 onions, chopped

2 shallots, finely chopped

4 garlic cloves, finely chopped

4 tablespoons soy sauce

$\frac{1}{4}$ teaspoon freshly ground black pepper

pinch of salt

2 teaspoons cornflour/cornstarch

Serves 4–6

Popular in the Southern states, these wings are basted and covered with a cola-based BBQ-style sauce. Serve with Blue Cheese Dipping Sauce (see page 29).

Preheat the oven to 180°C (350°F) Gas 4.

In a medium bowl, combine the brown sugar, cola or root beer, onions, shallots, garlic, soy sauce, pepper and salt.

Place the wings in a large, deep casserole or roasting dish. Pour over the cola mixture. Bake for 1½–2 hours or until the juices run clear when the thickest part is pierced to the bone. Turn the wings occasionally during cooking, to ensure they do not burn or brown too much.

Remove the wings from the dish and set aside.

Pour the soda mixture into a small saucepan and heat. Place the cornflour/cornstarch in a small bowl, add some of the warm sauce, and mix to form a loose paste. Pour this back into the pan with the remaining sauce and cook over a low-medium heat until the sauce has thickened to the desired consistency. Toss the wings in the sauce and serve with Blue Cheese Dipping Sauce.

Asian Caramel Wings

1.8 kg/4 lbs. chicken wings, halved at the joints, tips removed

vegetable oil, for frying

200 g/1 cup brown sugar

75 ml/¹⁄₃ cup fish sauce

75 ml/¹⁄₃ cup soy sauce

60 ml/¹⁄₄ cup orange juice

60 ml/¹⁄₄ cup freshly squeezed lime juice

Egg-fried Rice (see page 131), to serve

Green Onion Dipping Sauce:

250 ml/1 cup sour cream

225 g/1 cup mayonnaise

50 g/¹⁄₂ cup finely chopped spring onions/scallions

30 g/¹⁄₂ cup finely chopped fresh flat-leaf parsley

2 garlic cloves, finely chopped

1 teaspoon Dijon mustard

Serves 4–6

A sweet, yet savoury sauce that adds Asian flavours to the rich caramel. Fried and tossed, these wings have the perfect balance of delicate flavour and sweet seasoning. Serve with Green Onion Dipping Sauce.

Place the sugar in a medium saucepan with 60 ml/¹⁄₄ cup water over a medium-high heat and bring to a boil. Continue to boil and swirl (don't stir) for 6–7 minutes so the sugar caramelizes evenly.

Combine the fish sauce, soy sauce, orange juice, and lime juice with 60 ml/¹⁄₄ cup water in a cup. Once the caramel has turned a golden amber colour, slowly pour in the mixture and return to a boil. Continue to boil for 7 minutes until the sauce is well combined, then remove the sauce from the heat and keep warm.

Meanwhile, preheat the oil in a deep fryer to 180°C (350°F).

Fry the chicken wings in batches for about 10 minutes until cooked through and the juices run clear when the thickest part is pierced to the bone. Remove and drain on paper towels. Place in a large bowl, pour the caramel sauce over the wings and toss.

Serve with egg-fried rice on the side.

Green Onion Dipping Sauce

Mix all the ingredients together in a blender until smooth. Refrigerate before serving.

Spicy Thai-style Fried Wings

1.8 kg/4 lbs. chicken wings, halved at the joints, tips removed

9 garlic cloves

7.5-cm/3-in. piece of fresh ginger, peeled

6 tablespoons soy sauce

6 tablespoons curry paste

3 tablespoons rice vinegar

2 tablespoons coconut oil, melted

2 tablespoons runny honey

180 g/1^{1}/$_{3}$ cups plain/all-purpose flour

2 tablespoons cornflour/cornstarch

vegetable or canola oil, for frying

Lemongrass & Soy Dipping Sauce:

3 stalks of lemongrass

2 spring onions/scallions, chopped

1 teaspoon finely chopped garlic

1 teaspoon brown sugar

1 tablespoon sriracha sauce

3 tablespoons freshly squeezed lime juice

1 tablespoon fish sauce

2 teaspoons soy sauce

1 tablespoon chopped coriander/cilantro

1 tablespoon chopped basil

Serves 4–6

America has been on a fried chicken craze for a fair few years now. And let's be honest, fried chicken isn't so much a craze as it is a way of life. This recipe is spicy, crispy and perfect for anything from picnics to family parties and get-togethers.

Preheat the oil in a deep fryer to 180°C (350°F).

Chop the garlic and ginger by pulsing briefly in a food processor. Add the soy sauce, curry paste, vinegar, coconut oil and honey. Purée until smooth. Put the sauce into a bowl.

In a separate bowl, whisk the flour and cornflour/cornstarch with 350 ml/1^{2}/$_{3}$ cups water. Add the chicken and toss until well coated. Fry the chicken in about three batches, until golden, for 6–8 minutes until golden, then drain on paper towels.

Bring the oil back to 180°C (350°F) and fry the chicken for a further 6–8 minutes, until crisp and the juices run clear when the thickest part is pierced to the bone. Drain again, then toss the chicken in the sauce.

Serve with the Lemongrass & Soy Dipping Sauce (see below).

Lemongrass & Soy Dipping Sauce

Trim the ends of the lemongrass stalks and remove the outer layers, then finely chop. Place in a bowl with the other ingredients and 3 tablespoons water. Mix well, then chill in the refrigerator before serving.

Sake Wings

These oven-fried, Asian-inspired chicken wings are flavoured with reduced sake, teriyaki sauce, ginger and chilli/hot red pepper flakes. A teri-sake infusion!

1.8 kg/4 lbs. chicken wings, halved at the joints, tips removed

250 ml/1 cup soy sauce

120 ml/½ cup sake, dry sherry or dry white wine

3 tablespoons very finely chopped fresh ginger

1½ tablespoons finely chopped garlic

200 g/1 cup sugar

1½ teaspoons chilli/hot red pepper flakes

100 g/1 cup thinly sliced spring onions/scallions, (white and green parts), plus extra for garnishing

3½ tablespoons rice vinegar

3 tablespoons cornflour/cornstarch

2 tablespoons toasted sesame seeds

Serves 4–6

Plum Dipping Sauce:

1.3 kg/3 lbs. plums, pitted and chopped

4 garlic cloves, finely chopped

1 tablespoon finely chopped fresh ginger

1 small onion, finely chopped

200 g/1 cup brown sugar

2 tablespoons teriyaki sauce

1 teaspoon sesame oil

2 tablespoons soy sauce

½ teaspoon crushed dried chilli

freshly squeezed juice of 1 lemon

2 tablespoons cornflour/cornstarch

In a small saucepan, whisk together the soy sauce, sake (or sherry or white wine), ginger, garlic, sugar, chilli/hot red pepper flakes, spring onions/scallions, vinegar and cornflour/cornstarch with 3 tablespoons water. Set the pan over a medium heat and bring to a boil, whisking constantly (the mixture will be very thick). Let cool. If not using immediately, cover and refrigerate for up to 4 days.

Preheat the oven to 190°C (375°F) Gas 5. Grease 2-3 baking sheets with cooking spray or vegetable oil.

Add the sauce mixture to a large bowl with the wings and mix well. Arrange the wings and sauce in a single layer on the baking sheets.

Bake for 30 minutes. Stir and turn the wings over in the sauce, then bake for a further 20 minutes. Stir and turn the wings again and bake for a final 10 minutes, or until the chicken is tender and the juices run clear when the thickest part is pierced to the bone, and the sauce is thick and shiny. Stir the wings in the sauce and transfer to a serving platter. Spoon some of the extra sauce over, then sprinkle with the sesame seeds and onions.

Plum Dipping Sauce

Place all the ingredients except the cornflour/cornstarch in a medium saucepan with 475 ml/2 cups water. Bring to a boil, then reduce the heat and simmer for 30 minutes. Remove from the heat. Mix the cornflour/cornstarch with 1 tablespoon water, then pour into a blender with the plum mixture. Blend until combined. Pour back into the pan and cook on medium-low until the mixture thickens to the desired consistency.

Lime & Maple Wings

vegetable or canola oil, for frying

1.8 kg/4 lbs. chicken wings, halved at the joints, tips removed

250 ml/1 cup hot sauce, such as Frank's Red Hot® original hot sauce

250 ml/1 cup freshly squeezed lime juice

zest of 2 limes

3$\frac{1}{2}$ tablespoons maple syrup

75 g/5 tablespoons unsalted butter, melted

2 garlic cloves, crushed

1 teaspoon cayenne pepper

$\frac{1}{2}$ teaspoon freshly ground black pepper

Serves 4–6

At first glance, you may not think that maple syrup and lime would go well together, but they are actually a harmonious and flavourful combination. Fry these wings and toss them in a sticky, messy, zesty sauce.

Preheat the oil in a deep fryer set to 180°C (350°F).

Fry the chicken wings for about 10 minutes, until cooked and the juices run clear when the thickest part is pierced to the bone. Drain on paper towels.

Meanwhile, combine the hot sauce, lime juice, lime zest, maple syrup, butter, garlic, cayenne pepper and black pepper in a large bowl. As the wings finish cooking, transfer the sauce to a medium saucepan over a medium-low heat and heat through.

Place the cooked wings in a large bowl, pour the sauce over and toss to coat. Reserve any extra sauce for dipping.

These wings are also good with Ranch Dipping Sauce (see page 49).

Chocolate Wings

1.8 kg/4 lbs. chicken wings, halved at the joints, tips removed

1 tablespoon vegetable oil

4 garlic cloves, chopped

2 tablespoons chilli powder

$^1/_2$ teaspoon ground allspice

$^1/_4$ teaspoon ground cloves

500 ml/2 cups passata/ strained tomatoes

115 g/4 oz. dark/bittersweet chocolate, coarsely chopped

1 teaspoon hot sauce, such as Tabasco

$^1/_2$ teaspoon salt

cooked rice, garnished with spring onions/scallions and coriander/cilantro

Chocolate Ketchup:

1 quantity of Homemade Ketchup (see page 74)

$^1/_8$ teaspoon ground cinnamon

100 g/$3^1/_2$ oz. cooking chocolate, chopped into pieces and melted in the microwave

Serves 4–6

This is the recipe for all chocolate lovers! This chocolate chicken makes a great dinner for a romantic night in. Chocolate and chicken might not seem an obvious partnership, but this sauce – a combination of chocolate, tomato sauce, cloves and other spices – shows how it can be done. Serve with homemade Chocolate Ketchup.

Heat the oil in a large, heavy-based frying pan/skillet over a medium-high heat. Add the chicken wings in several batches and cook for 5 minutes, turning occasionally, until browned. Remove from the pan and set aside.

Reduce the heat under the pan to medium. Add the garlic, chilli powder, allspice and cloves and cook, stirring, for 1 minute. Stir in the tomato sauce, scraping up the browned bits from the base of the pan. Add 250 ml/1 cup water, the chocolate, hot sauce and salt and cook, stirring, until the chocolate has melted.

Return the wings to the pan and lower the heat. Cover and simmer for about 25 minutes until the wings are cooked through and the juices run clear when the thickest part is pierced to the bone, and the sauce is reduced to a thick glaze. Serve with Chocolate Ketchup (see below) and rice with chopped spring onions/scallions and coriander/cilantro.

Chocolate Ketchup

Place the Homemade Ketchup in a medium saucepan over a medium heat and bring to a simmer. When the mixture has been warmed thoroughly, stir in the cinnamon and melted chocolate. When well mixed together, remove from the pan and refrigerate before serving.

Peanut Butter & Jelly Wings

240 g/2 cups plain/
all-purpose flour

$^1/_2$ teaspoon salt

$^1/_2$ teaspoon freshly ground
black pepper

1.8 kg/4 lbs. chicken wings,
halved at the joints, tips
removed

300 g/1 cup grape jam/jelly
(redcurrant jam/jelly also
works well)

225 g/1 cup smooth peanut
butter

2 tablespoons soy sauce

2 tablespoons sriracha
sauce, plus extra for
serving

roasted peanuts, chopped

vegetable or canola oil, for
frying

Grape Jelly Dipping
Sauce:

150 g/$^1/_2$ cup grape
jam/jelly

150 g/$^1/_2$ cup plain or vanilla
yogurt

Serves 4–6

Peanut butter and jelly is probably one of the most successful and popular flavour combinations. It might not initially seem plausible that these two condiments would go with chicken, but go ahead and try it – they really do make the perfect combination.

In a medium bowl, combine the flour, salt and pepper. Toss the chicken wings in the seasoned flour to coat lightly. Shake off the excess.

In a small pan, combine the grape jam/jelly, peanut butter, soy sauce, and sriracha sauce with 60 ml/$^1/_4$ cup water. Cook over a low heat, stirring until the sauce is smooth. Keep warm until needed.

Preheat the oven to 180°C (350°F) Gas 6. Line 2–3 baking sheets with foil and grease lightly with cooking spray or vegetable oil.

Preheat the oil in a deep fryer to 180°C (350°F).

Fry the chicken wings in batches for 10–12 minutes until they are golden brown and cooked through and the juices run clear when the thickest part is pierced to the bone.

Drain the wings and transfer to a large bowl. Toss the wings with the sauce, then arrange on the baking sheets. Bake in the preheated oven for 5 minutes. Serve the wings immediately with chopped peanuts and extra sriracha sauce on top.

Grape Jam/Jelly Dipping Sauce

Heat the jam/jelly in a small saucepan over a low heat. When mixture is smooth, mix the warmed jelly with the yogurt. Serve immediately.

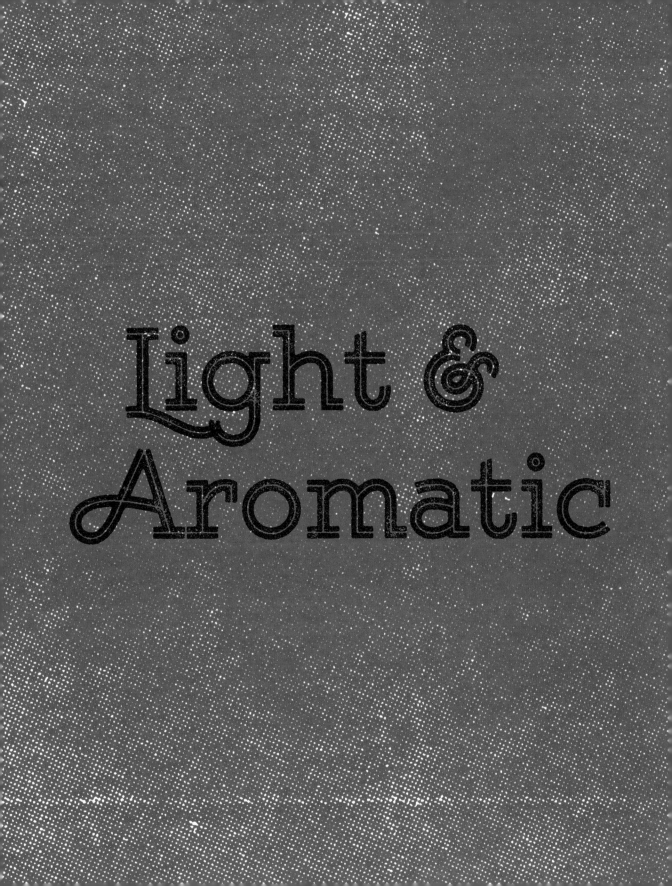

Light & Aromatic

Baked Pistachio Wings

1.8 kg/4 lbs. chicken wings, halved at the joints, tips removed

2 tablespoons vegetable or canola oil

60 g/$\frac{1}{2}$ cup sweet paprika

$\frac{1}{2}$ teaspoon sea salt

3 tablespoons garlic powder

3 tablespoons freshly ground black pepper

3 tablespoons ground ginger

3 tablespoons onion powder

1 teaspoon dried rosemary, chopped

80 g/6 tablespoons unsalted butter

1 garlic clove, finely chopped

125 g/1 cup pistachios, toasted and finely crushed

500 ml/2 cups runny honey

$\frac{1}{2}$ teaspoon sriracha sauce

Greek yogurt, for dipping

Serves 4-6

These wings are almost too delicious to be considered healthy! With a sweet, honey-pistachio sauce, these wings are salty, sweet and almost healthy, all at the same time. The coated wings need to marinate for several hours, so start this recipe in good time.

Put the wings in a large bowl, add the oil and mix together until the wings are thoroughly coated.

Combine the paprika, sea salt, garlic powder, black pepper, ground ginger, onion powder and rosemary in a small bowl.

Line 2–3 baking sheets with paper towels, and place a wire rack on each.

Add the spice rub to the bowl of wings and toss to coat well. Place the coated wings on the wire racks, cover with clingfilm/plastic wrap and refrigerate for 3 hours or overnight.

When ready to bake the wings, preheat the oven to 225°C (425°F) Gas 7.

Remove the paper towels from the baking sheets. Keep the wings on the wire racks. Bake in the preheated oven for 20 minutes, then turn the wings over and bake for a further 10 minutes, until golden brown and the juices run clear when the thickest part is pierced to the bone.

Mix the butter, garlic, pistachios, honey and sriracha together in a small saucepan over a low heat. When warmed and combined, pour over the wings and bake for another 10 minutes.

These wings are good dipped into Greek yogurt.

Baked Parmesan Wings

When baked, these wings have the flavour and crispiness of fried chicken, without the decadence of fried food. They are very versatile and can be enjoyed with a variety of dipping sauces.

90 ml/^{1}/$_3$ cup balsamic vinegar

50 g/^{1}/$_4$ cup salt

1 bay leaf

1 teaspoon dried thyme

1 teaspoon dried oregano

1 teaspoon dried rosemary

1.8 kg/4 lbs. chicken wings, halved at the joints, tips removed

7 garlic cloves, finely chopped

3 tablespoons olive oil

1 tablespoon freshly ground black pepper

2 teaspoons chilli/hot red pepper flakes, or to taste

50 g/^{1}/$_4$ cup fine breadcrumbs

60 g/1 cup finely grated Parmesan

Serves 4-6

Homemade Ketchup:

500 g/18 oz. tomato purée/paste

120 ml/^{1}/$_2$ cup white wine vinegar or apple cider vinegar

1 teaspoon garlic powder

1 tablespoon onion powder

2 tablespoons sugar

2 tablespoons molasses or treacle

1 teaspoon sea salt

1 teaspoon mustard powder

^{1}/$_8$ teaspoon each of cinnamon, cloves, allspice and cayenne pepper

1 teaspoon powdered chia seeds, for thickness (optional)

Pizza Dipping Sauce:

250 ml/1 cup passata/strained tomatoes

1 tablespoon Italian seasoning

2 teaspoons dried oregano

1 teaspoon garlic powder

Preheat the oven to 230°C (450°F) Gas 7. Line 2-3 baking sheets with foil and grease with cooking spray or vegetable oil.

Combine the vinegar, salt, bay leaf, thyme, oregano and rosemary with 1.5 litres/6^1/$_2$ cups water in a large saucepan and bring to a boil. Add the chicken wings, return to the boil and cook for 15 minutes. Using a slotted spoon, transfer the wings to a cooling rack and allow to dry for 15 minutes.

Mash the garlic with a pinch of salt in a pestle and mortar until smooth. Combine the mashed garlic, olive oil, black pepper and chilli/hot red pepper flakes in a large bowl. Add the breadcrumbs, then the chicken wings and toss to coat. Sprinkle with half the cheese. Transfer to the prepared baking sheets and sprinkle with the remaining cheese.

Bake in the preheated oven for 20-25 minutes, until golden and the juices run clear when the thickest part is pierced to the bone.

Serve with Homemade Ketchup or Pizza Dipping Sauce (see below).

Homemade Ketchup

Put all the ingredients in a blender or food processor with 250 ml/1 cup water and blend well. Chill in the refrigerator overnight or for at least 2 hours.

Pizza Dipping Sauce

Simmer the passata/strained tomatoes with the seasonings for about 20 minutes, then let cool.

Lemon, Basil & Pepper Wings

1.8 kg/4 lbs. chicken wings, halved at the joints, tips removed

2 tablespoons freshly ground black pepper

3 tablespoons freshly squeezed lemon juice

2 teaspoons seasoned salt

$1^1/2$ teaspoons smoked paprika

1 teaspoon garlic powder

$^1/2$ teaspoon chilli/hot red pepper flakes

2 tablespoons chopped fresh basil

4 tablespoons olive oil

3 tablespoons grated lemon zest

lemon wedges, to serve

Garlic–Cream Dipping Sauce:

120 g/$^1/2$ cup plain yogurt

120 ml/$^1/2$ cup sour cream

100 g/$^1/2$ cup mayonnaise

8 garlic cloves, or to taste, finely chopped

$^1/4$ teaspoon paprika

$^1/2$ teaspoon salt

$^1/4$ teaspoon freshly ground black pepper

fresh chives, finely chopped

Serves 4–6

This might be the healthiest recipe in this book. With three primary ingredients, it's easy to mix and match and dabble with the flavouring. In any event, these wings are delicious in winter when citrus is in season, or in summertime when it gives a refreshing zing.

Combine all the ingredients except the lemon zest in a large bowl. Toss until the wings are thoroughly coated. Cover the bowl with clingfilm/plastic wrap and marinate in refrigerator overnight (or for at least 4 hours).

Preheat the oven to 200°C (400°F) Gas 6.

Line 2–3 baking sheets with foil.

Arrange the wings on the baking sheets and pour the leftover marinade over them. Bake for about 30 minutes or until the wings are golden brown on each side and the juices run clear when the thickest part is pierced to the bone.

Remove the wings from the oven and let cool briefly. Sprinkle with lemon zest and fresh basil leaves and serve with lemon wedges.

Garlic–Cream Dipping Sauce

Mix all the ingredients except the chives together until smooth and well combined. Chill until ready to serve, then garnish with chives.

Greek Olive & Feta Wings

These chicken wings have a refreshing Mediterranean feel to them. Using a mixture of breadcrumbs, Greek olives and feta, this combination of flavours makes a wonderfully satisfying dish.

80 g/½ cup Greek olives, stoned/pitted and diced, plus a few whole olives to garnish

3 tablespoons freshly squeezed lemon juice

2 tablespoons olive oil

2 tablespoons runny honey

1 teaspoon dried oregano

1 garlic clove, finely chopped

¼ teaspoon salt

1.8 kg/4 lbs. chicken wings, halved at the joints, tips removed

225 g/3 cups panko breadcrumbs

80 g/½ cup crumbled feta cheese

Mint-Cream Dipping Sauce:

250 g/1 cup plain Greek yogurt

freshly squeezed juice of 1 lime

3 garlic cloves, crushed

30 g/1 cup fresh mint leaves, finely chopped, plus extra to garnish

¼ teaspoon cayenne pepper

1 teaspoon ground cumin

1 teaspoon paprika

1 teaspoon ground coriander

salt

Serves 4–6

Combine the olives, lemon juice, oil, honey, oregano, garlic and salt in a large resealable bag. Add the chicken wings, seal the bag and toss to coat. Refrigerate overnight or for at least 4 hours.

Preheat the oven to 200°C (400°F) Gas 6. Line 2–3 baking sheets with foil.

Pour the panko crumbs into a medium bowl.

Remove the wings from marinade, roll in the panko crumbs and arrange the wings on the baking sheets. Discard the remaining marinade. Bake for 35-40 minutes until golden and the juices run clear when the thickest part is pierced to the bone. Garnish with the whole olives and the crumbled feta.

Mint-Cream Dipping Sauce

Mix all the ingredients together in a bowl until smooth and creamy.

Boneless Baked Chicken Fillets

1.8 kg/4 lbs. chicken fillets/tenders

130 g/1 cup plain/all-purpose flour

1 teaspoon cayenne pepper

1 teaspoon garlic powder

1 teaspoon salt

170 g/^{3}/4 cup butter, melted

150 ml/^{3}/4 cup hot pepper sauce, such as Frank's Red Hot®

Honey-Chipotle Dipping Sauce:

340 g/1^1/4 cups runny honey

120 ml/^{1}/2 cup tomato ketchup (or Homemade Ketchup, see page 74)

1^1/2 tablespoons white wine vinegar

1 tablespoon ground chipotle chilli powder

^{3}/4 teaspoon salt

Serves 4–6

Boneless wings are for those who don't like to deal with chicken bones – or those of you who sometimes eat pizza with a knife and fork! These wings are bone-free, baked until crispy and served with a honey-chipotle sauce, although almost any sauce and marinade from this book would work with this baked chicken.

Line 2–3 baking sheets with foil, and lightly grease with cooking spray or vegetable oil.

Place the flour, cayenne pepper, garlic and salt in a resealable plastic bag and shake to mix. Add the chicken, seal the bag and toss until well coated with the flour mixture.

Place the chicken on the lined baking sheets. Cover loosely with clingfilm/plastic wrap and place in the refrigerator for at least 1 hour.

Preheat the oven to 200°C (400°F) Gas 6.

Whisk together the melted butter and hot sauce in a small bowl. Dip the wings into the butter mixture, then place back on the baking sheets. Bake in the preheated oven for 25–30 minutes, until the chicken is crispy on the outside and the juices run clear when the thickest part is pierced to the bone. Turn the wings over halfway during cooking so they cook evenly.

Honey-Chipotle Dipping Sauce

Combine all the ingredients in a medium saucepan with 120 ml/^{1}/2 cup water and bring to a boil over a medium-high heat. Reduce the heat once the mixture comes to a boil and let simmer for 3–5 minutes.

Extra-crunchy Crumbed Wings

1.8 kg/4 lbs. chicken wings, halved at the joints, tips removed

500 ml/2 cups buttermilk (optional)

4 large eggs, beaten

100 g/³/₄ cup sesame seeds

100 g/³/₄ cup plain/all-purpose flour

1 tablespoon coarse salt

¹/₂ teaspoon cayenne pepper

250 g/4 cups fresh breadcrumbs

4 garlic cloves, finely chopped

Soy-Caramel Dipping Sauce:

75 g/¹/₃ cup sugar

4–5 large shallots, chopped

1 garlic clove, finely chopped

¹/₂ tablespoon finely chopped fresh ginger

3 tablespoons soy sauce

3 tablespoons rice vinegar (not seasoned)

2 tablespoons cornflour/cornstarch

1 tablespoon freshly squeezed lemon juice (optional)

Serves 4–6

These wings are the perfect combination of textures – tender, soft meat enclosed in a crisp, herbed coating.

If using buttermilk, put the wings and buttermilk in a medium bowl and cover. Refrigerate overnight, or for at least 4 hours.

Preheat the oven to 190°C (375°F) Gas 5. Line 2–3 baking sheets with baking parchment, or grease with oil.

Remove the wings from the buttermilk and discard. Place the wings in a large bowl, add the eggs and toss to coat.

Combine the sesame seeds, flour, salt, cayenne pepper, breadcrumbs and garlic in a small bowl. Dip each wing into the sesame mixture to fully coat. Place the coated wings side by side on the baking sheets.

Bake in the preheated oven for 30 minutes, then increase the oven temperature to 200°C (400°F) Gas 6. Cook for a further 20–30 minutes, until the wings are golden brown and sizzling, and the juices run clear when the thickest part is pierced to the bone. Remove the wings from the baking sheets and serve with the dipping sauce.

Soy-Caramel Dipping Sauce

Cook the sugar in a large, dry, heavy-based saucepan over a medium-high heat, undisturbed, until it melts around edges and begins to turn a perfect golden colour.

Add the shallots (use caution as the caramel will bubble up and steam vigorously) and cook for about 45 seconds, stirring, until the shallots shrink and become fragrant. Add the garlic and ginger and cook, stirring, for 30 seconds. Stir in the soy sauce, vinegar, and 335 ml/1¹/₃ cups water and simmer for 1 minute, stirring, until any hardened caramel has dissolved. The sauce will become a rich auburn colour.

Mix the cornflour/cornstarch with 2 tablespoons water until smooth, then stir into the sauce and simmer for 2 minutes, stirring occasionally. Remove from the heat and plunge the pan into a sink of cold water to stop the caramel cooking. If using lemon juice, stir it in now. Cover the sauce and keep warm.

Strawberry Balsamic Wings

1.8 kg/4 lbs. chicken wings, halved at the joints, tips removed

450 g/2 cups strawberry jam/jelly, plus extra for brushing on the cooked wings

250 ml/1 cup freshly squeezed lemon juice

250 ml/1 cup balsamic vinegar

3$\frac{1}{2}$ tablespoons smoked paprika

1$\frac{1}{4}$ tablespoons salt

French Fries (see page 120), to serve

Serves 4–6

These chicken wings have a deliciously sweet yet savoury, sticky taste to them. The char of the grill combines well with the strawberry and balsamic flavours. These are perfect on a warm spring evening, when the BBQ season hasn't quite arrived!

Whisk the strawberry jam/jelly, lemon juice, balsamic vinegar, paprika and salt together in a medium saucepan over a low heat. When combined, remove from the heat and let cool.

Place the chicken wings in a large resealable plastic bag and pour in the cooled sauce. Seal the bag shut, squeezing out as much air from the bag as possible. Marinate the wings in the refrigerator overnight or for at least 2 hours.

Take the chicken out of the refrigerator 30 minutes before cooking, to let it to come to room temperature.

Preheat the grill/broiler or a grill pan to medium-low heat.

Grill the chicken wings for 7–10 minutes per side, or until the wings are cooked through and the juices run clear when the thickest part is pierced to the bone.

Remove the wings from the heat, and brush them on both sides with more jam/jelly. Serve immediately with a side of French Fries.

Blackberry & Red Wine Wings

780 g/6 cups blackberries (or 450 g/2 cups blackberry jam or preserve), plus extra for garnishing

60 g/4 tablespoons butter

2 onions, finely chopped

500 ml/2 cups (or a half bottle) Pinot Noir red wine

60 ml/¼ cup freshly squeezed lemon juice

150 g/½ cup seedless blackberry jam/jelly

2 teaspoons coarsely ground black pepper

2 teaspoons salt

1.8 kg/4 lbs. chicken wings, halved at the joints, tips removed

Serves 4–6

These chicken wings are pure summertime, with a marinade made from fresh blackberries (although jam/jelly can be substituted if blackberries are not in season). The freshness of the berries mixed with a fruity Pinot Noir give these wings a sweet taste.

Put the blackberries in food processor or blender and purée. Push the berries through a fine mesh sieve/strainer into a small bowl. Set aside.

Heat the butter in a small saucepan over medium-low heat. Add the onions and sauté for about 10 minutes, stirring occasionally, until tender and pale yellow. Add the red wine and lemon juice. Bring to a boil; then lower the heat and simmer until reduced by about half.

Combine the blackberry pulp, jam/jelly, pepper and salt in a small bowl, then add to the wine mixture. Bring to a boil, then reduce the heat and simmer for 5 minutes. Remove from the heat, cover and cool in the refrigerator for a few hours.

Place half the sauce in a large, resealable plastic bag. Add the chicken wings to the bag and tightly seal, squeezing as much air from the bag as possible as you do so. Marinate the wings in the refrigerator overnight or for at least 2 hours.

Take the chicken out of the refrigerator 30 minutes before cooking, to let it to come to room temperature.

Preheat the grill/broiler or a grill pan to a medium-low heat.

Grill the chicken wings for 7–10 minutes per side, or until the wings are cooked through and the juices run clear when the thickest part is pierced to the bone.

Remove the wings from the heat, and brush them on both sides with the remaining sauce. Serve immediately.

Green Tea Wings

Green tea leaves are used to spice the wings, giving an earthy hint to an otherwise Asian-flavoured recipe. The green tea dipping sauce makes the perfect accompaniment.

60 ml/^{1}/4 cup soy sauce

3 tablespoons rice wine vinegar

165 g/^{1}/2 cup runny honey

2 tablespoons grated fresh ginger

2 garlic cloves, finely chopped

6 spring onion/scallion greens, finely sliced

2 tablespoons chilli/hot red pepper flakes

50 g/^{1}/4 cup brown sugar

10 g/^{1}/4 cup loose-leaf green tea leaves

2 star anise

12 coriander seeds

1.8 kg/4 lbs. chicken wings, halved at the joints, tips removed

edamame beans, to serve

Green Tea Dipping Sauce:

300 ml/1^1/4 cups sour cream

1 tablespoon loose-leaf green tea

1 spring onion/scallion, finely chopped (green parts only)

Serves 4–6

Combine all the ingredients, except the chicken and the edamame beans, in a bowl. Place two-thirds of this mixture in a large resealable bag; set aside the remaining third.

Add the chicken wings to the resealable bag and toss to coat. Refrigerate overnight or for at least 4 hours.

Preheat the oven to 200°C (400°F) Gas 6. Line 2–3 baking sheets with foil.

Remove the wings from the marinade and arrange on the lined baking sheets. Discard the marinade left in the bag.

Baste the wings with the reserved marinade. Bake in the preheated oven for 35–40 minutes, re-basting the wings with remaining sauce after 20 minutes, until the juices run clear when the thickest part is pierced to the bone. Serve with edamame beans.

Green Tea Dipping Sauce

Combine the sour cream and green tea leaves in a small bowl, then set aside for 1 hour. Add the spring onion/scallion just before serving.

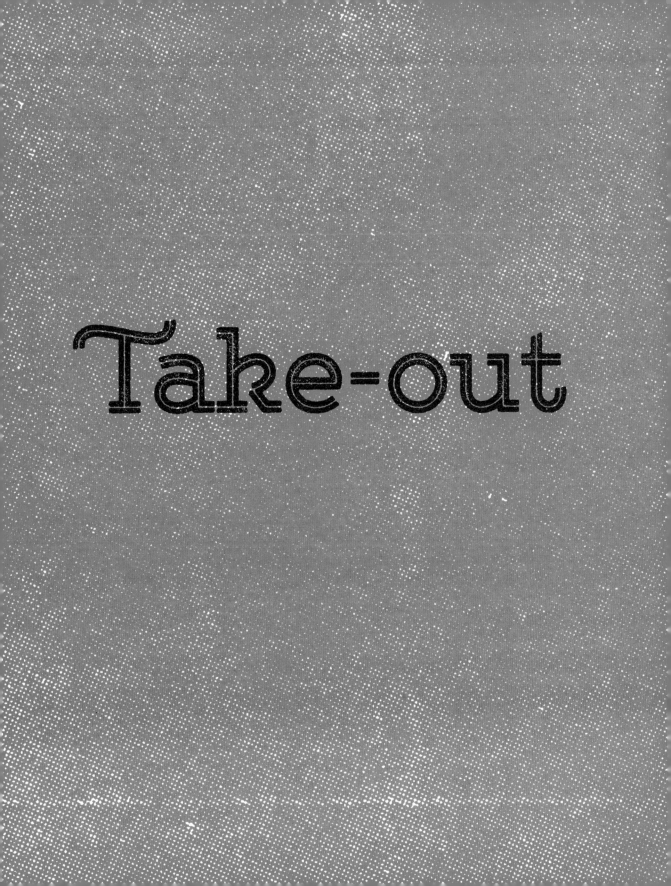

Take-out

General Tso's Slow-cooker Wings

1.8 kg/4 lbs. chicken wings, halved at the joints, tips removed

5 teaspoons finely chopped garlic

8 tablespoons runny honey

2 teaspoons grated fresh ginger

6 tablespoons soy sauce

1 teaspoon crushed chilli/hot red pepper flakes

225-g/9-oz. mangetout/sugar snap peas, cooked

slow cooker

Serves 4–6

Probably one of the most popular Chinese take-out dishes, General Tso's chicken has a Chinese BBQ sauce, sweetened with a combination of garlic, honey and ginger. The marinade is thick and pairs perfectly with darker chicken meat. Baked in a slow cooker, the meat falls right off the bone.

Place the chicken in the slow cooker.

Mix the remaining ingredients, except the mangetout/sugar snap peas, in a bowl. Pour this mixture over the chicken and stir.

Cook on high for 3–5 hours (adjust according to your slow cooker's settings, if necessary). Add the mangetout/sugar snap peas during the final 30 minutes of cooking and stir to coat with the sauce.

These wings go well with Ranch Dipping Sauce (see page 49).

Szechuan-Plum Sauce Wings

1.8 kg/4 lbs. chicken wings, halved at the joints, tips removed

1 kg/2 lbs. purple plums, stoned/pitted and chopped

50 g/¼ cup sugar

4 tablespoons hoisin sauce

3 tablespoons orange zest

1 tablespoon orange juice

2 tablespoons soy sauce

2 teaspoons grated fresh ginger

½ teaspoon freshly ground black pepper

Soy Dipping Sauce:

60 ml/¼ cup soy sauce

60 ml/¼ cup sour cream

1 tablespoon rice wine vinegar

1 tablespoon finely sliced spring onions/scallions

Serves 4-6

This recipe combines baked wings with a spicy plum sauce. It's sweet, with accompanying rich, deep flavours.

Preheat the oven to 190°C (375°F) Gas 5. Line 2–3 baking sheets with foil.

Place the plums, sugar, hoisin sauce, orange zest, orange juice, soy sauce, ginger and pepper in a blender or food processor and blend until nearly smooth.

Transfer the plum mixture to a medium saucepan. Bring to a boil, then reduce the heat. Simmer, uncovered, for about 15 minutes or until slightly thickened, stirring occasionally. When thickened, remove from the heat and divide into two. Set one half of the sauce aside.

Place the wings in a single layer on the baking sheets. Brush with the sauce, then turn them over and brush again. Bake for 25–30 minutes, turning them halfway through the cooking time and brushing with more sauce. The chicken should be thoroughly cooked and the juices run clear when the thickest part is pierced to the bone. Discard any remaining sauce that has been used for brushing the chicken.

In a small saucepan bring the remaining sauce to a boil, then transfer to a small bowl. Arrange the wings on a serving plate and serve with the warmed plum sauce and Soy Dipping Sauce (see below).

Soy Dipping Sauce

Combine all the ingredients in a blender or food processor, then chill in the refrigerator before serving.

Kung Pao Wings

120 ml/$\frac{1}{2}$ cup white wine

120 ml/$\frac{1}{2}$ cup soy sauce

4 tablespoons sesame oil,

50 g/$\frac{1}{2}$ cup cornflour/ cornstarch, dissolved in 120 ml/$\frac{1}{2}$ cup water

1.8 kg/4 lbs. chicken wings, halved at the joints, tips removed

85 g/3 oz. hot chilli paste

1$\frac{1}{2}$ tablespoons distilled white vinegar

3 tablespoons brown sugar

4 spring onions/scallions, chopped, plus extra to garnish

4 garlic cloves, finely chopped

450-g/16-oz. can water chestnuts, drained and sliced

100 g/1 cup chopped peanuts

1 fresh red chilli/chile, sliced, to garnish

Serves 4–6

These hot and spicy Chinese chicken wings are sautéed in a pan for tender meat and a sweet and sticky sauce. Serve with rice or pasta and dip in Sweet & Sour Sauce (see page 23) or Soy Dipping Sauce (see page 94).

Combine 4 tablespoons of the wine, 4 tablespoons of the soy sauce, 2 tablespoons of the sesame oil and 4 tablespoons of the cornflour/ cornstarch mixture in a bowl and mix together. Place the wings in a large, resealable plastic bag. Add the marinade, seal the bag and toss to coat. Place in the refrigerator to marinate overnight, or for at least 4 hours.

In a small bowl combine the remaining wine, soy sauce, oil and cornflour/cornstarch mixture with the chilli paste, vinegar and sugar. Mix together and add the chopped onion, garlic, water chestnuts and peanuts. Transfer the mixture to a medium sauté pan/skillet and heat the sauce slowly until aromatic.

Meanwhile, remove the chicken from the marinade and sauté in a second large sauté pan/skillet until meat is cooked through and the juices run clear when the thickest part is pierced to the bone. When the sauce is aromatic, add the sautéed chicken to it and let it simmer together until the sauce thickens, then serve immediately. Garnish with the sliced chilli/chile and spring onion/scallion.

Thai Green Curry Wings

2 tablespoons plain/all-purpose flour

2 teaspoons salt

2 teaspoons ground coriander

1.8 kg/4 lbs. chicken wings, halved at the joints, tips removed

5 tablespoons green chilli sauce (either hot or mild, depending on your taste)

4 tablespoons unsalted butter, melted

1 tablespoon fish sauce

2 teaspoons Thai green curry paste

3 tablespoons chopped fresh coriander/cilantro, to garnish

1 fresh red chilli/chile, sliced, to garnish

Coconut Cream Dipping Sauce:

400-g/16-oz. can of coconut milk

225 g/1 cup brown sugar

Serves 4–6

Of all the curries, Thai green curry seems to have the most flavour and aroma. Here, chicken wings are baked with a spicy green curry sauce that is perfect when served over rice.

Preheat the oven to 200°C (400°F) Gas 6. Line 2–3 baking sheets with foil and grease with cooking spray or vegetable oil.

In a bowl, mix the flour with the salt and ground coriander. Add the chicken and toss to coat. Spread the chicken on the baking sheets in a single layer and sprinkle with vegetable oil.

Roast the chicken in the preheated oven for 45 minutes, turning once or twice, until browned and crispy and the juices run clear when the thickest part is pierced to the bone.

In a bowl, whisk together the chilli sauce, butter, fish sauce and curry paste. Add the cooked chicken wings to the sauce and toss. Sprinkle with the chopped coriander/cilantro and serve with Coconut Cream Dipping Sauce.

Coconut Cream Dipping Sauce

Combine the ingredients in a medium saucepan and bring to a boil over a medium-high heat. Reduce the heat to medium-low and cook, stirring, for about 20 minutes until the mixture is thick and the volume has reduced by about half.

Coconut Curry Wings

85 g/$\frac{1}{2}$ cup coconut oil

4 teaspoons Jamaican/
Caribbean curry powder

4 teaspoons garlic powder

1 teaspoon ground ginger

generous pinch of salt and
freshly ground black
pepper

1.8 kg/4 lbs. chicken wings,
halved at the joints, tips
removed

vegetable oil, for frying

1 cucumber (English) and
1 radish, chopped into
chunks, for garnishing

handful of coriander/
cilantro, chopped, for
garnishing

Coconut Curry Sauce:

2 tablespoons coconut oil

1 garlic clove, crushed and
finely chopped

2 tablespoons freshly grated
ginger

2 tablespoons Jamaican/
Caribbean curry powder

1 teaspoon crushed
chilli/hot red pepper
flakes

400 ml/1$\frac{3}{4}$ cups coconut
milk

3 tablespoons runny honey

2 tablespoons soy sauce

freshly squeezed juice of
2 limes, plus a squeeze for
serving

couple of pinches of nutmeg

Serves 4–6

These chicken wings are fried and then tossed in a flavoursome coconut-curry sauce. This dish goes perfectly with rice or naan bread, and makes a delicious weeknight dinner.

Combine the coconut oil, curry powder, garlic, ginger, salt and pepper together in a small saucepan and heat gently until the coconut oil has melted. Slather on the wings and place in a large resealable plastic bag. Place in the refrigerator and marinate for at least 4 hours.

Preheat the oil in a deep fryer set to 180°C (350°F).

Preheat the oven to 200°C (400°F) Gas 6. Line 2–3 baking sheets with foil.

Fry the wings, a few at a time, for 6–8 minutes until they are golden brown. Place the fried wings on the baking sheets and bake in the preheated oven for 5 minutes for extra crispness or until the juices run clear when the thickest part is pierced to the bone.

Once the wings are done, toss with sauce in a large mixing bowl. Garnish with the cucumber and radish chunks and a squeeze of lime before serving.

Coconut Curry

Combine the coconut oil with the garlic, ginger, curry powder and chilli/hot red pepper flakes in a medium saucepan and cook gently for 2 minutes. Add the coconut milk, honey, soy sauce, lime juice and nutmeg. Bring to a light simmer and let it reduce for 40–45 minutes until it reaches a thicker consistency.

Thai Peanut Wings

1.8 kg/4 lbs. chicken wings, halved at the joints, tips removed

4 garlic cloves, finely chopped

225 g/1 cup smooth peanut butter

120 ml/$\frac{1}{2}$ cup freshly squeezed lemon juice

1 tablespoon crushed chilli/hot red pepper flakes, plus extra for garnishing

1$\frac{1}{2}$ tablespoons ground cumin

kosher/flaked salt, to taste

fresh flat-leaf parsley, chopped

cucumber wedges, to serve

Serves 4–6

These chicken wings are grilled/broiled for extra crispness and served with a warm peanut sauce. They are sweet, yet savoury and full of flavour.

Whisk together the garlic, peanut butter, lemon juice, crushed chilli/ hot red pepper flakes and ground cumin with 250 ml/1 cup warm water; season with salt.

Toss the chicken wings with 225 g/1 cup of the sauce, cover and marinate in the refrigerator overnight or for at least 2 hours.

Preheat the grill/broiler. Grill/broil the chicken, for 20–25 minutes, turning occasionally, until cooked through, lightly charred and the juices run clear when the thickest part is pierced to the bone.

Serve the wings with the remaining sauce, topped with chopped parsley and crushed chilli/hot red pepper flakes, accompanied by cucumber wedges.

Teriyaki Wings

350 ml/1^1/$_2$ cups soy sauce

300 g/1^1/$_2$ cups sugar

175 ml/^{3}/$_4$ cup pineapple juice

120 ml/^{1}/$_2$ cup vegetable oil

2 garlic cloves, finely chopped

1^1/$_2$ tablespoons finely chopped fresh ginger

1.8 kg/4 lbs. chicken wings, halved at the joints, tips removed

Green Onion–Ranch Dipping Sauce:

225 ml/1 cup sour cream

225 g/1 cup mayonnaise

35 g/^{1}/$_2$ cup finely chopped spring onions/scallions

1 tablespoon finely chopped fresh flat-leaf parsley

1 garlic clove, finely chopped

1 teaspoon Dijon mustard

Serves 4–6

These oven-baked teriyaki wings are marinated in a tangy pineapple-based teriyaki sauce. Serve with Green Onion–Ranch Dipping Sauce.

Combine the soy sauce, sugar, pineapple juice, vegetable oil, garlic and ginger in a large bowl with 350 ml/1½ cups water. Mix until the sugar has dissolved. Pour the marinade into a large resealable plastic bag. Add the wings and marinate in the refrigerator overnight or for at least 4 hours.

Preheat the oven to 180°C (350°F) Gas 5. Line 2–3 baking sheets with foil.

Remove the chicken from the marinade and arrange on the baking sheets. Brush with the remaining marinade. Bake for about 1 hour, or until the juices run clear when the thickest part is pierced to the bone. Serve with the dipping sauce below.

Green Onion–Ranch Dipping Sauce

Combine the ingredients in a blender until smooth.

Jerk Wings

These caramelized jerk chicken wings are spicy, juicy and very, very moreish, and the Cajun Remoulade Dipping Sauce makes the perfect accompaniment.

1.8 kg/4 lbs. chicken wings, halved at the joints, tips removed

1/2 onion, chopped

35 g/1/2 cup spring onions/scallions, sliced

7 garlic cloves, finely chopped

4 habanero peppers, deseeded and chopped

3 tablespoons chopped fresh thyme leaves

2 teaspoons dried thyme

2 tablespoons kosher/flaked salt

1 tablespoon freshly ground black pepper

1 tablespoon ground allspice

1 teaspoon ground cinnamon

2 teaspoons ground cumin

1 teaspoon chilli powder

1 teaspoon freshly grated nutmeg

4 tablespoons vegetable oil

5 tablespoons soy sauce

3 tablespoons brown sugar

120 ml/1/2 cup freshly squeezed lime juice

Cajun Remoulade Dipping Sauce:

500 g/2 cups mayonnaise

2 tablespoons Homemade Ketchup (see page 74)

2 tablespoons English mustard

1 tablespoon chopped fresh flat-leaf parsley

1 tablespoon cayenne pepper

1 tablespoon freshly squeezed lemon juice

2 teaspoons prepared horseradish

3 garlic cloves, finely chopped

1 teaspoon Worcestershire sauce

1 teaspoon celery salt

1 teaspoon paprika

Serves 4–6

Put the onion, spring onions/scallions, garlic, habanero peppers, fresh and dried thyme, kosher salt, black pepper, allspice, cinnamon, cumin, chilli powder, nutmeg, vegetable oil, soy sauce, brown sugar and lime juice in a blender and blend until the marinade is completely smooth.

Place the chicken in a large bowl, pour the marinade over and toss to coat completely. Cover the bowl with clingfilm/plastic wrap and marinate in the refrigerator overnight or for at least 8 hours.

Preheat the oven to 230°C (450°F) Gas 8. Line 2–3 baking sheets with foil and grease with cooking spray or vegetable oil.

Place the chicken on the baking sheets and reserve the marinade left in the bowl. Bake in the preheated oven for 25 minutes.

Brush half the reserved marinade over the chicken and turn the wings over. Bake for a further 15 minutes.

Turn the chicken again and brush on the remaining marinade. Bake for a further 10–15 minutes until the chicken is tender and caramelized and the juices run clear when the thickest part is pierced to the bone. Rest the wings on the baking sheets for 5 minutes before transferring to a serving platter.

Cajun Remoulade Dipping Sauce

Combine all ingredients in a blender or food processor. Refrigerate before serving.

Cajun Alfredo Wings

1.8 kg/4 lbs. chicken wings, halved at the joints, tips removed

4 tablespoons olive oil

Cajun Spice Mix:

2 tablespoons garlic powder

2 tablespoons freshly ground black pepper

1 tablespoon kosher/flaked salt

1$\frac{1}{2}$ tablespoons ground cumin

1$\frac{1}{2}$ tablespoons onion powder

1 teaspoon cayenne pepper

2 teaspoons Italian seasoning

2 teaspoons smoked paprika

1$\frac{1}{2}$ teaspoons chilli powder

Alfredo Dipping Sauce:

60 g/4 tablespoons butter

4 garlic cloves, finely chopped

850 ml/4 cups whipping cream

$\frac{1}{2}$ teaspoon freshly ground black pepper

75 g/1 cup grated/shredded Parmesan cheese

200 g/ 1$\frac{1}{2}$ cups grated/shredded mozzarella

Serves 4–6

These chicken wings, although very similar to the jerk recipe on the previous page, are just a smidge less hot and celebrate the fusion of the American South with Italian and French cooking. The rich Alfredo Dipping Sauce is the perfect match for these wings.

Coat the wings in 2 tablespoons of the olive oil and set aside.

Combine all the spices for the Cajun Spice mixture in a large, resealable plastic bag and shake to mix. Add the wings to the bag, shake to coat in the spice mixture, then place in the refrigerator to marinate overnight.

Preheat the grill/broiler to medium. Line a baking sheet with foil. Arrange the wings on the sheet and place under the grill/broiler. Grill/broil for 10 minutes on each side or until thoroughly cooked and the juices run clear when the thickest part is pierced to the bone.

Serve the wings with the Alfredo Dipping Sauce.

Alfredo Dipping Sauce

In a medium saucepan over a medium heat, combine the remaining olive oil with the butter and garlic and cook until the garlic becomes aromatic. Add the cream and pepper and bring to a simmer, stirring often. Let the sauce thicken to desired consistency – this will take 30–40 minutes. Remove from the heat and stir in the cheese.

Cacciatore Wings

1.8 kg/4 lbs. chicken wings, halved at the joints, tips removed

salt and freshly ground black pepper

130 g/1 cup plain/all-purpose flour

4 tablespoons olive oil

60 g/4 tablespoons butter

1 medium onion, sliced

1 red (bell) pepper, deseeded and chopped

1 yellow (bell) pepper, deseeded and chopped

6 garlic cloves. finely chopped

280 g/4 cups mushrooms, chopped

475 ml/2 cups red wine

1 bay leaf

1 1/2 tablespoons dried oregano

1/2 teaspoon ground turmeric

2 x 400-g/14-oz. cans chopped tomatoes

cooked penne pasta, to serve

Parmesan cheese, grated/shredded, to serve

basil leaves, to garnish

Serves 4–6

This baked recipe combines tomatoes, peppers and Italian spices to create a beautifully rich Italian-inspired chicken wing dish.

Preheat the oven to 200°C (400°F) Gas 6.

Season the chicken wings with salt and pepper and dredge with flour, shaking off the excess.

Heat the oil and butter in a large, deep ovenproof sauté pan/skillet and fry the chicken wings on both sides. Remove the chicken from the pan/skillet.

Add the onion, peppers, garlic and mushrooms to the pan/skillet and cook for a few minutes. Add the wine, bay leaf, oregano and turmeric and cook for a couple more minutes.

Add the tomatoes, stir well and cook for 5 minutes, then return the chicken to the pan. Cover the pan, place in the oven and bake for 45–60 minutes or until the juices run clear when the thickest part of the chicken is pierced to the bone.

This dish is good served over penne pasta or rice and with Alfredo Dipping Sauce on the side (see page 109).

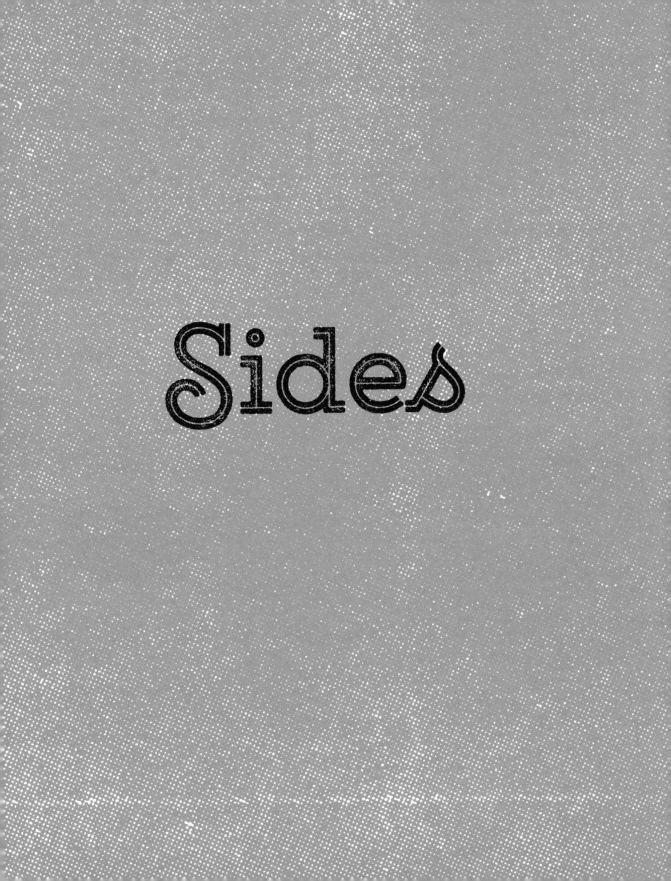

Sides

Crispy Pickled Vegetables

450 g/3 cups pickling
  cucumbers, sliced into
  chips

450 g/1 lb. baby carrots,
  halved lengthwise

1 fennel bulb, cored and cut
  into 5 x 1-cm/2 x ¹/₂-in.
  matchsticks

1 red (bell) pepper, cut
  into 5 x 1-cm/2 x ¹/₂-in.
  matchsticks

450 g/1 lb. green or pole
  beans, cut into 5-cm/2-in.
  lengths

450 g/1 lb. celery, cut into
  5 x 1-cm/2 x ¹/₂-in.
  matchsticks

1 chilli/chile of your choice,
  cut into thin strips
  (optional, for heat)

700 ml/3 cups cider vinegar

120 ml/¹/₂ cup white wine
  vinegar

150 g/³/₄ cup sugar

1 tablespoon kosher/flaked
  salt

1 teaspoon coriander seeds

1¹/₂ teaspoons black
  peppercorns

1 tablespoon fresh ginger,
  cut into matchsticks

1 bay leaf

9 garlic cloves, crushed

muslin/cheesecloth

Makes 2–3 jars

These spicy, crispy pickled vegetables make the perfect accompaniment to wings and their sauces and dips. They bring a sour flavour to some of the recipes, making a good contrast to some of the sweeter sauces. These are delicious raw, fried or served as an accompaniment to a Bloody Mary.

Combine all the vegetables, except the chilli, if using, in a large, deep bowl or pan.

In a medium heatproof bowl, cover the chilli/chile, if using, with boiling water and let stand for about 10 minutes until softened. Drain and transfer to a large saucepan.

Add the cider vinegar, white wine vinegar, sugar, salt, coriander seeds, peppercorns, ginger, bay leaf and garlic. Add 700 ml/3 cups water and bring to a boil, stirring to dissolve the sugar.

Cover the top of the bowl containing the vegetables with muslin/cheesecloth, then pour the hot liquid over the contents. Ball up the sifted spices in the muslin/cheesecloth, tie to keep together and submerge in the pickling mixture. Cover the vegetables/pickling liquid with a plate to keep the vegetables submerged. Let cool to room temperature, then cover with clingfilm/plastic wrap and refrigerate for 2–3 days.

Drain the vegetables and transfer to a large serving platter. Alternatively, transfer the vegetables to sterilized jars and top up with the pickling liquid. They'll keep in the fridge for up to 2 weeks.

Beer-battered Onion Rings

375 g/3 cups plain/
all-purpose flour

2 eggs, separated

250 ml/1 cup beer (such as
IPA, Pilsner or German
lager)

60 g/4 tablespoons butter,
melted and cooled

salt and freshly ground
black pepper

3 large yellow or white
onions, sliced into rings

vegetable oil, for frying

Serves 4–6

Crispy, beer-battered onion rings are the ideal accompaniment for chicken wings. Serve up a sampling of onion rings and fried mozzarella sticks (see page 127) along with the chicken wings of your choice for a perfect sharing platter.

Sift the flour into a large bowl. Set aside one-third of the flour for dredging the onions.

In a separate, large bowl, whisk the egg yolks. Mix in the beer, melted butter and salt and pepper. Slowly stir the egg yolk and beer mixture into the bowl containing two-thirds of the flour and mix well. Allow the mixture to stand for 30-60 minutes.

Preheat the oil in a deep fryer set to 180°C (350°F).

In a small bowl, beat the egg whites until stiff peaks are formed. Fold the egg whites into the batter. Coat each onion ring with flour, then dip into the batter. Fry several at a time, until golden brown.

Elotes

vegetable oil, for brushing

1 teaspoon chilli powder

$1/2$ teaspoon cayenne pepper

8 corn on the cob/ears of corn

50 g/$1/4$ cup mayonnaise or unsalted butter

40 g/$1/2$ cup crumbled Cotija, Parmesan or ricotta salata cheese

1 lime, cut into 8 wedges

Serves 8

This Mexican street food pairs well with many of the wing recipes in this book. Cotija is a hard, crumbly Mexican cheese, but Parmesan or ricotta work just as well.

Build a medium-hot fire in a charcoal grill or preheat a grill/broiler to medium-high and brush the grill rack with oil. Combine the chilli powder and cayenne pepper in a small bowl.

Grill/broil the corn for about 10 minutes, turning occasionally with tongs, until cooked through and lightly charred. Remove from the grill and brush each ear with $1/2$ teaspoons of mayonnaise or butter. Sprinkle each with a tablespoon of cheese and a pinch of the chilli-cayenne mixture. Squeeze a lime wedge over each corn on the cob/ear of corn and serve.

Alternatively, remove the corn kernels from the cob, after taking them off the grill, and combine the corn with the mayonnaise or butter and the cheese. Top with the chilli-cayenne mixture and a dash of lime juice.

French Fries

1.1 kg/2½ lbs. russet or baking potatoes, peeled

130 g/1 cup plain/all-purpose flour

1 teaspoon garlic salt

1 teaspoon onion salt

1 teaspoon salt

1 teaspoon paprika

1 teaspoon cayenne pepper, Ranch Seasoning (see page 49) or other seasoning of your choice (optional)

125 ml/½ cup beer or water, or more as needed

vegetable oil, for frying

Serves 4–6

There is no better accompaniment to chicken wings, burgers and other decadent foods than French fries. Dunk them in any one of the dipping sauces in this book or sprinkle with extra salt.

Slice the potatoes into French fries and place into a big bowl of cold water (this prevents them turning brown while the oil is heating).

Preheat the oil in a deep fryer set to 180°C (350°F).

While the oil is heating, mix the flour, garlic salt, onion salt, regular salt and paprika (and other seasonings, if using) in a large bowl with a whisk. Gradually stir in enough beer or water so that the mixture can be drizzled from a spoon.

Dip the fries in the batter one at a time, and carefully lower into the hot oil so they are not touching at first (the fries need to be placed into the fryer one at a time, or they will clump together). Fry until golden brown and crispy. Remove and drain on paper towels. Serve with a dipping sauce of your choice.

Bourbon Baked Beans

450 g/1 lb. bacon, cut into
2.5-cm/1-in. pieces

1 onion, chopped

3 x 440-g/16-oz. cans
baked beans

440-g/16-oz. can kidney
beans, drained

2 tablespoons dark
molasses or treacle

2 tablespoons dark brown
sugar

80 ml/⅓ cup bourbon

120 ml/½ cup chilli sauce

1 teaspoon mustard powder

1 teaspoon ground
cinnamon

Serves 6–8

These baked beans are made with a mixture of pre-baked beans from a can and kidney beans. The dark brown sugar, dark molasses and bourbon give the beans a smoky, sweet flavour. These pair well with many of the chicken wing recipes and can be baked in the oven alongside the wings.

Preheat the oven to 180°C (350°F) Gas 4.

Cook the bacon on a baking sheet in the oven or in a frying pan/skillet on the stovetop until crisp. Drain and set aside, saving the bacon drippings.

Sauté the onion in the bacon drippings until translucent.

In a large bowl, mix the onion, baked beans, kidney beans, molasses, sugar, bourbon, chilli sauce, mustard and cinnamon. Add the bacon and fold in gently.

Pour the mixture into a large pot or casserole dish. Cover with a lid or with foil. Bake the beans for 40 minutes, then let stand for 10–15 minutes before serving.

Pimento Macaroni Cheese

240 g/2 cups dried
 macaroni

60 g/4 tablespoons butter

3 tablespoons plain/
 all-purpose flour

1 teaspoon mustard powder

530 ml/2¼ cups milk

115 g/1¼ cups
 mature/sharp Cheddar
 cheese, grated/shredded

115 g/1¼ cups mild
 Cheddar cheese,
 grated/shredded

5 dashes of hot sauce

115-g/4-oz. jar pimentos,
 drained

kosher/flaked salt

freshly ground black pepper

Serves 4–6

This mac and cheese is a classic and reminds me of my father, who loved pimento cheese. Add leftover chicken wings, ham or bacon for an added kick.

Preheat the oven to 180°C (350°F) Gas 4.

Fill a large saucepan with water, and bring to a rolling boil. Add 1 tablespoon salt and the macaroni to the water. Cook for 5 minutes, then drain and set aside.

In the same saucepan, melt the butter over a medium heat. Add the flour, and whisk constantly for about 3 minutes, until the flour mixture is a light amber colour. Add the mustard powder. Slowly whisk in the milk, and continue to whisk over a medium heat for about 5 minutes or until the sauce has thickened. Remove from the heat and add the grated/shredded cheese and a few dashes of hot sauce, whisking until the cheese has melted. Season with salt and pepper to taste.

Add the pasta back into the saucepan with the cheese sauce and toss to coat. Stir in the drained pimentos.

Pour into a medium baking dish. Cover with foil and bake in the preheated oven for about 30 minutes, then remove the foil and bake for a further 10 minutes uncovered, until starting to brown on top and bubbling around the edges.

Deep-fried Mozzarella Cheese Sticks

2 eggs, beaten

120 g/1½ cups Italian-seasoned breadcrumbs or breadcrumbs with a tablespoon of Ranch Seasoning (see page 49)

½ teaspoon garlic salt

80 g/⅔ cup plain/all-purpose flour

40 g/⅓ cup cornflour/cornstarch

450-g/1-lb. bag of mozzarella cheese sticks

vegetable oil, for frying

Serves 4–6

Warm, crispy, gooey cheese sticks are a great companion to chicken wings. Serve these mozzarella sticks with an array of the dips or sauces in this book.

In a small bowl, mix the eggs with 60 ml/¼ cup water.

In a separate, medium bowl, mix the breadcrumbs and garlic salt. In another medium bowl, mix the flour and cornflour/cornstarch.

Preheat the oil in a deep fryer set to 180°C (350°F).

One at a time, coat each mozzarella stick in flour, then egg and then breadcrumbs. Fry for about 30 seconds until golden brown. Drain on paper towels before serving.

Potato & Egg Salad

4 medium red potatoes

3 hard-boiled eggs, chopped

50 g/^{1}/$_4$ cup chopped celery

50 g/^{1}/$_4$ cup chopped spring
   onions/scallions

1 red (bell) pepper, chopped

1 tablespoon Dijon–Blue
   Cheese Dipping Sauce
   (see page 12) or hot, sweet
   or Dijon mustard

100 g/^{1}/$_2$ cup mayonnaise
   or mascarpone cheese

salt and freshly ground
   black pepper

paprika, to garnish
   (optional)

2 tablespoons finely
   chopped fresh dill

Serves 4–6

This cold salad was inspired by a suggestion from my
sister, Kelly, and it has turned out to be one of the best
side dishes I've ever tasted.

Cook the potatoes in boiling salted water until tender when pierced
with a fork. Drain and set aside until cool enough to handle. With the
skin still on, cut the potatoes into bite-sized pieces and place in a
bowl. Add the eggs, celery, spring onions/scallions and (bell) pepper.

Mix the dipping sauce or mustard in a separate small bowl with the
mayonnaise or mascarpone. Gently mix into the potato salad. Season
with salt, pepper and add the dill. Sprinkle paprika over the top before
serving, if desired.

Garlic-roasted Baby Potatoes

1.5 kg/3 lbs. small red new
   potatoes or baby potatoes,
   washed and halved

60 ml/^{1}/$_4$ cup olive oil

1 teaspoon salt

1 teaspoon freshly ground
   black pepper

Serves 6

These potatoes are quick, easy, cheap and delicious.
The salt-roasted skins gives the dish a nice, crisp
texture that doesn't skimp on flavour.

Preheat the oven to 230°C (450°F) Gas 8. Line a large baking sheet
with foil.

Toss the potatoes with the oil, salt and pepper and arrange, cut-side
down, on the lined baking sheet. Roast in the preheated oven for
20–30 minutes until golden and brown, turning halfway through.
Toss with more salt before serving, if so desired.

Summer Rolls

60 g/2 oz. rice vermicelli

8 rice wrappers (22-cm/
8.5-in. diameter)

3 tablespoons chopped fresh
mint leaves

3 tablespoons chopped fresh
coriander/cilantro

2 lettuce leaves, chopped

1½ tablespoons fish sauce

2 tablespoons lime juice

2 garlic cloves, finely
chopped

1½ tablespoons white sugar

½ teaspoon garlic-chilli sauce

2 tablespoons hoisin sauce

1 teaspoon finely chopped
peanuts

Makes 8

These refreshing, fragrant rolls are the perfect
accompaniment to many recipes in this book.

Bring a medium saucepan of water to boil. Boil the rice vermicelli for
3–5 minutes, or until al dente, and drain.

Fill a large bowl with warm water. Dip one wrapper into the hot water
for 1 second to soften. Lay the wrapper flat. In a row across the centre,
place a handful of vermicelli, mint, coriander/cilantro and lettuce,
leaving about 5 cm/2 in. uncovered on each side. Fold the uncovered
sides inward, then tightly roll the wrapper, beginning at the end with
the lettuce. Repeat with remaining ingredients.

In a small bowl, mix the fish sauce, 4 tablespoons water, lime juice,
garlic, sugar and chilli sauce. In another small bowl, mix the hoisin
sauce and peanuts. Serve immediately with the Summer Rolls.

Egg-fried Rice

2½ tablespoons vegetable oil

80 g/¾ cup finely chopped
onion

2 eggs, lightly beaten

2 chicken wings, shredded

2 tablespoons light soy sauce

pinch of salt

60 g/½ cup julienned carrots

80 g/½ cup pineapple
chunks

500 g/4 cups cold, cooked
medium-grain rice

4 spring onions/scallions,
chopped

115 g/2 cups beansprouts

Serves 4–6

A fantastic side for Take-out section recipes!

In a medium pan or wok, over a medium heat, add a little oil and sweat
the onions. Remove from pan and set aside. Meanwhile, beat the eggs in
a bowl with a pinch of salt and a splash of soy sauce. Add a little more
oil to the pan and add the eggs, scrambling. When cooked through,
remove from pan and let cool, chop into small pieces.

Add 1 more tablespoon of oil to
the pan, add the chicken, carrots,
pineapple and cooked onion,
cook on a medium heat for about
2 minutes. Add the rice, spring
onions/scallions and
beansprouts, toss to mix and
cook for another 2–3 minutes.
Add the 2 tablespoons of soy
sauce and chopped egg to the rice
mixture and fold in. Cook for 1
minute more and serve at once!

Guacamole

6 avocados, peeled, stoned/
pitted and mashed

juice of 2 limes

2 teaspoons salt

1 large onion, diced

5 tablespoons chopped
fresh coriander/cilantro

4 plum tomatoes, diced

2 teaspoons finely chopped
garlic

cayenne pepper, to taste

There is something addictive about guacamole. Its refreshing flavour and creaminess makes it the perfect match for not just crunchy corn or tortilla chips, but also for salads, sandwiches and chicken wings!

In a large bowl, combine and mash together the avocados, lime juice and salt. When incorporated, mix in the onion, coriander/cilantro, tomatoes and garlic. Stir in cayenne pepper to taste and add more salt if needed. Refrigerate for 1 hour before serving for the best flavour.

Salsa

3 large tomatoes, chopped

1 green (bell) pepper,
chopped

1 red onion, diced

20 g/^{1}/$_4$ cup finely chopped
fresh coriander/cilantro

2 tablespoons lime juice

^{1}/$_2$–1 jalapeño pepper, finely
chopped

^{1}/$_2$ teaspoon ground cumin

1 teaspoon flaked salt

1 teaspoon black pepper

This delicious salsa can be served with tortilla chips and chicken wings, or poured over crispy, baked or fried wings for a south-of-the-border flavoured snack.

Combine all the ingredients in a bowl. Serve immediately or cover and refrigerate until required.

Salsa Verde

225-g/8-oz. can of tomatillos,
drained, or fresh

^{1}/$_2$ small onion, chopped

1 garlic clove, finely chopped

1 fresh green chilli/chile,
finely chopped

2 tablespoons chopped fresh
coriander/cilantro

^{1}/$_4$ teaspoon ground cumin

1 teaspoon salt, or to taste

This accompaniment is tasty, spicy and hot, and goes well with guacamole.

Combine all the ingredients in a saucepan with 250 ml/1 cup water. Bring to a boil over a high heat, then reduce the heat to medium-low and simmer for 10–15 minutes until the tomatillos are soft. Purée the mixture in a blender until smooth (you may need to do this in batches). Serve immediately or cover and refrigerate until required.

All dips serve 6–8

Buttermilk Waffles

220 g/1³/₄ cups plain/
all-purpose flour

2 teaspoons baking powder

1 teaspoon baking soda/
bicarbonate of soda

1 tablespoon sugar

¹/₂ teaspoon salt

3 UK large, US extra large
eggs, at room
temperature

1 teaspoon vanilla extract

350 ml/1¹/₂ cups
buttermilk, at room
temperature

115 g/1 stick unsalted
butter, melted and cooled

waffle iron

Makes 4

In the US, especially in the south, waffles are often served with chicken wings. These waffles are fluffy due to their buttermilk base and are fantastic served with chicken or slathered with maple syrup for breakfast (or for dessert!). As a variation, you can stir grated Cheddar cheese into the batter just before cooking.

Heat up the waffle iron according to the manufacturer's instructions.

In a large batter bowl, combine the flour, baking powder, baking soda/bicarbonate of soda, sugar and salt, stirring well to combine the ingredients. Create a depression in the centre of the dry ingredients.

Beat the eggs in a large measuring cup or medium bowl until frothy and well combined. Add the vanilla extract, buttermilk and cooled butter. Beat until well combined.

Pour the buttermilk mixture into the dry ingredients' depression and stir rapidly with a wooden spoon until well combined. There will be an immediate chemical reaction between the buttermilk and the dry ingredients, creating a thick, rich batter honeycombed with air bubbles.

Using the wooden spoon, push one quarter of the batter onto your waffle-iron plates and bake according to the waffle iron instructions or until the steam stops rising from the waffle iron.

Coconut Cookies

340 g/2½ cups self-raising/self-rising flour, plus extra for dusting

pinch of salt

2 tablespoons sugar

85 g/1 cup sweetened desiccated/shredded coconut, plus 2 tablespoons for sprinkling

115 g/1 stick cold butter, cut into 1-cm/½-in. pieces

120 g/½ cup plain yogurt

150 ml/¾ cup cold buttermilk

2 tablespoons butter, melted

Makes 12

A sweet treat that complements a variety of spicy chicken wing flavours.

Mix the flour, salt, sugar and coconut together in a medium bowl.

Cut the cold butter into the flour mixture, using a pastry cutter or two knives, until the butter is in pea-sized pieces; leave some pieces a little larger.

Stir in the yogurt and buttermilk until just mixed, adding a little extra buttermilk or yogurt if the mixture feels dry. Wrap in clingfilm/plastic wrap and chill in the refrigerator for 20 minutes.

Preheat the oven to 200°C (400°F) Gas 6. Butter a 23-cm/9-in. round or square cake pan.

Turn the dough out onto a work surface lightly dusted with flour. Gently roll or flatten the dough to a thickness of about 2 cm/¾ in. Using a 5–7-cm/2–3-in. cookie cutter, cut out the cookies by pressing straight down with the cutter (do not twist).

Gather the scraps and re-roll again, this time to a thickness of 2.5 cm/1 in. and cut out as many cookies as you can.

Place the cookies in the buttered cake pan. Brush the tops of the biscuits with melted butter and sprinkle with the remaining coconut.

Bake the cookies in the preheated oven for 10 minutes, then lower the temperature to 190°C (375°F) Gas 5. Cover the cookies loosely with foil if the coconut is browning too much. Bake for a further 5–10 minutes. The cookies are done when the tops are golden brown. Serve warm.

Sodas & Cocktails

Homemade Root Beer

115 g/1/2 cup sassafras root
bark

small bunch of mint leaves

zest of 1 lime

1 vanilla pod/bean, split and
seeds scraped out

1 cinnamon stick

pinch of ground coriander

pinch of allspice

200 g/1 cup sugar

85 g/1/4 cup molasses

Serves 4-6

Homemade root beer is one of the most refreshing
drinks, especially in summertime. Pair with vanilla ice
cream for a root beer float, or use as a base for BBQ
sauce, marinades or dips to accompany chicken wings.

Put the sassafras root bark and mint in a large saucepan. Add the
lime zest, vanilla (seeds and pod), cinnamon, ground coriander and
allspice. Add 700 ml/3 cups water. Bring to a boil, then reduce the heat
and a simmer for 15–20 minutes until the mixture reduces by a third.

Strain through a fine mesh sieve/strainer into a large jug/pitcher.
While still warm, add the sugar and molasses and stir until dissolved.

To serve, dilute 1–2 tablespoons of the syrup with 225 ml/1 cup
soda water.

Homemade Cola

400 g/2 cups white sugar

2 tablespoons dark brown
sugar

zest of 1 very large or
2 small/medium oranges

zest of 1 lime

zest of 1 lemon

2 teaspoons coriander
seeds, crushed in a pestle
and mortar

1 1/2 teaspoons dried
lavender

4 star anise

1 vanilla pod/bean, split

1 cinnamon stick

1 teaspoon finely chopped
fresh ginger,

1/4 teaspoon citric acid

Serves 4-6

This homemade cola recipe is a perfect non-alcoholic
accompaniment to just about anything and everything
in this book. Combine the ingredients and cook down to
create a syrup that, when combined with soda water,
equals the classic taste of homemade soda-pop.

Place all the ingredients in a medium saucepan with 450 ml/2 cups
water. Over a medium heat, boil for 20 minutes, then remove from the
heat and set the pan in a large bowl of ice.

To serve, dilute 1–2 tablespoons of the syrup with 225 ml/1 cup
soda water.

Homemade Lemon-Lime Soda

400 g/2 cups sugar

2 limes, sliced

2 lemons, sliced

mint leaves (optional)

Serves 4–6

This refreshing homemade soda combines citrus and sugar with soda water, making a drink very similar to sparkling lemonade. Add mint for extra refreshment.

In a medium saucepan, combine the sugar, lemons and limes with 450 ml/2 cups water. Bring to a boil over a medium heat and boil for 5 minutes. Remove from heat and let cool, then strain.

To serve, dilute 1–2 tablespoons of the syrup with 225 ml/1 cup soda water.

Homemade Strawberry Soda

400 g/2 cups sugar

900 g/2 lbs. strawberries

ice cubes, to serve

Serves 4–6

Strawberry soda is the perfect refreshment during spring and summertime. If your strawberries are sweet or perfectly ripe, halve the amount of sugar.

Place strawberries in a heavy-based saucepan, add 450 ml/2 cups water and bring to a boil. Stir, then reduce the heat to low and simmer for about 15 minutes, until the strawberries soften.

Strain the juice into a separate saucepan, using a fine mesh sieve/strainer. Discard the strawberry pulp. Stir in the sugar until it dissolves, then bring strawberry juice back to a boil. Reduce the heat to medium and simmer for 5 minutes. Skim any foam from the top of the syrup. Remove from the heat and let cool to room temperature.

Pour the syrup into a lidded container and refrigerate.

To serve, dilute 1–2 tablespoons of the syrup with 225 ml/1 cup soda water.

Spiced Cream Soda

Cream soda is one of the most delicious, refreshing and not to mention, sweet sodas out there. This one is a spicier take on a cream soda, lending a bit of a kick to the regular cream soda flavour most of us are used to. Serve with ice cream or with spiced rum for an adult drink.

400 g/2 cups sugar

$\frac{1}{2}$ teaspoon citric acid

$\frac{1}{2}$ tablespoon molasses

1 tablespoon almond extract

1 tablespoon vanilla extract

Serves 4–6

Fruit & Spice Blend:

75 g/$\frac{1}{2}$ cup dried plums/prunes

75 g/$\frac{1}{2}$ cup raspberries

7.5-cm/3-in. piece of vanilla pod/bean, split

1 tablespoon wintergreen leaves (or juniper berries if wintergreen is unavailable)

$\frac{1}{2}$ tablespoon whole cloves

6 star anise

1 teaspoon ginger paste

1 teaspoon ground nutmeg

$\frac{1}{2}$ teaspoon ground cardamom

$\frac{1}{2}$ teaspoon ground cinnamon

In a saucepan, combine the fruit and spice blend ingredients with 450 ml/2 cups water. Bring to a boil, then remove from the heat and let steep for 30–60 minutes.

Strain out the solid ingredients and return the water to the saucepan. Add the sugar, citric acid, and molasses and heat until dissolved. Remove the syrup from the heat.

Chill the syrup and add the almond and vanilla extracts. Dilute with soda water to serve.

Avocado Margarita

This avocado margarita provides a savoury spin on a beloved tequila cocktail. The salt on the rim brings out the spice and citrus in the drink.

$\frac{1}{2}$ teaspoon chilli powder

1 lime, cut into wedges, plus extra to garnish

2 ripe avocados, stoned/pitted and peeled

450 g/3 cups ice

180 ml/$\frac{3}{4}$ cup freshly squeezed lime juice

1$\frac{1}{2}$ teaspoons agave nectar

250 ml/1 cup tequila

125 ml/$\frac{1}{2}$ cup Triple Sec

3 sprigs of fresh coriander/cilantro (optional)

1 tablespoon sea salt

Serves 4–6

Combine all the ingredients, except the salt, in a blender and blend until icy and smooth.

Place the sea salt on a plate. Dampen the rims of the glasses, then dip them in the salt. Pour in the margaritas and serve with lime wedges on the side.

Moonshine Punch

This is not a real 'moonshine' punch. Real moonshine is made in garages, barns and closets all over the world, but it's technically illegal in many areas. This version uses whiskey as its base. It's a woozy cocktail, so enjoy with caution.

450 ml/2 cups Jack Daniels

1 tablespoon lemon-lime syrup (see page 142)

1 tablespoon root beer syrup (see page 141)

1 tablespoon cola syrup (see page 141)

700 ml/3 cups soda water

225 ml/1 cup orange juice

Serves 4–6

Combine all the ingredients and serve over ice.

Peach Iced Tea

200 g/1 cup sugar

3 ripe peaches, stoned/
   pitted and thinly sliced

2 litres/8 cups filtered
   water

2-3 tablespoons loose-leaf
   black or green tea (3-4 tea
   bags), depending how
   strong you prefer it

Serves 4–6

The star of this drink is the peach syrup. This syrup can not only be used for iced tea, but also for a peach soda when combined with soda water.

Place the sugar and peaches in a small saucepan with 250 ml/1 cup water. Bring to a boil, then lower the heat and use a wooden spoon to stir and crush the peaches to infuse the water with their flavour.

Once the sugar has dissolved, remove the saucepan from the heat, cover and let steep for 20 minutes. Strain the syrup into a sterilized jar and refrigerate.

To serve, boil the filtered water and brew the tea in a large teapot, then place in the refrigerator to cool. Add 1–2 tablespoons of peach syrup to 250 ml/1 cup unsweetened tea or soda water.

Spiked Sweet Tea

6-8 tea bags, black or green

200 g/7 oz. loosely packed
   fresh mint leaves

115 g/$\frac{1}{2}$ cup plus
   1 tablespoon sugar

250 ml/1 cup lemon-lime
   syrup (see page 142)

250 ml/1 cup vodka,
   bourbon or spiced dark
   rum

lemon slices, to garnish

mint leaves, to garnish

Serves 4–6

This sweet tea recipe adds lemon-lime syrup and alcohol for a refreshing adult beverage. It can be served over ice or blended.

Bring 700 ml/3 cups water to a boil in a large saucepan. Remove from the heat and add the tea bags and mint. Stir in the sugar, cover and let steep for 12 minutes.

Remove the tea bags and mint. Stir in the lemon-lime syrup, 1 litre/ 4 cups water and the alcohol. Serve garnished over ice.

Beer Margarita

350-ml/12-oz can 'frozen' limeade concentrate or 350 ml/1^{1}/$_{2}$ cups homemade limeade concentrate (see below)

350 ml/1^{1}/$_{2}$ cups tequila

350 ml/1^{1}/$_{2}$ cups beer

1 tablespoon sea salt

ice, to serve

1 lime, cut into wedges

Homemade Limeade Concentrate:

300 g/1^{1}/$_{2}$ cups sugar

350 ml/1^{1}/$_{2}$ cups freshly squeezed lime juice

Serves 4

One part beer and one part margarita, this adult-only beverage is a great drink for groups of friends. The limeade makes this drink refreshing and the perfect thirst quencher for a big game or relaxing weekend outside in the garden/backyard.

If making the limeade concentrate, put the sugar into a saucepan with 350 ml/1^{1}/$_{2}$ cups water. Heat gently over a low heat, stirring occasionally, until the sugar has dissolved. Add the lime juice and stir well. Let cool, then freeze.

To make the beer margarita, combine the limeade, tequila and beer in a large jug/pitcher with 350 ml/1^{1}/$_{2}$ cups water, Stir until the limeade has melted and everything has combined.

Place the sea salt on a plate. Dampen the rims of the glasses, then dip them in the salt.

Pour over ice and garnish with a lime wedge.

Origins of the Buffalo Wing

Chicken wings are synonymous with sports in America. Come football season, Americans spend many hours cheering on their hometown with a cold brew in hand and fingers covered in sticky wing sauce mixed with blue cheese. For a few short months, the chicken wing becomes the most expensive and sought-after part of the chicken.

However, most of us have no idea how this food delicacy became such a hit. Just 50 years ago, the chicken wing was considered one of the least edible parts of a chicken, something that cooks and homemakers only salvaged into making chicken stock. This fact brings up two mystifying questions about the chicken wing: How did this become one of America's favourite food pastimes and why is it named after a burly animal that wandered the American frontier.

Well, the 'buffalo' part of the name refers to the city in Upstate New York. Not a relative of the bison. Besides the chicken wing, Buffalo – the 69th largest city in the U.S. – doesn't have too much more to distinguish itself from many other cities in western New York, although it's really quite an interesting town from its vast blue-collar history to its close proximity to the Niagara Falls.

In the 1980s, Calvin Trillin, a well-respected journalist for *The New Yorker* came to the conclusion that Buffalo, New York was indeed the capital of all things chicken wings and he explored the history in-depth and also taste-tested at many of the chicken wing-touting restaurants in the region.

So where and why did the chicken wing become the buffalo wing? In almost all accurate accounts, it came from a stroke of ingenuity in 1964 from a woman named Teressa Bellissimo, owner of the Anchor Bar in Buffalo, New York.

Teressa's husband, Frank tells the story that the invention of the chicken wing, like so many other wonderful inventions, evolved due to a mistake. The couple, who founded the Anchor Bar in 1939 say that one afternoon, instead of getting their regular old chicken neck delivery, which they used in their spaghetti sauce, wings were delivered to the bar instead. To avoid wasting the wings, Frank asked Teressa to concoct a bar appetizer; the result was the delectable, spicy dish we all know, love and hold dear to our hearts today.

However, Teressa and Frank's son, Dom, gives a more specific account.

According to him, it was a late Friday night, right at the end of Lent. Some of the regulars had been very diligent about keeping to their religious requirements of eating fish and vegetables, but still came into the bar to blow off some steam from work and home life. Dom asked his mother to make something special for these regulars that had been spending a lot of money during this time of year – something that they could pass around 'gratis' at the stroke of midnight. Dom agrees with his father's version of events that chicken wings had been delivered to the bar instead of the necks, but claimed that his business-minded mother looked at the wings and must have thought 'perfect' – meat so unusable that it could be given away for free to the local barflies. Little did she know that the Buffalo chicken wing would go from being a unheralded, wasted part of the chicken to her one and only culinary claim to fame.

Both Frank and Dominic agreed on a few other crucial details, namely that Teressa cut each wing in half to produce a 'drumstick' and a 'flat', that she deep-fried them without breading and covered them in a hot sauce, and that she served them with celery (from the house antipasto) and a blue cheese salad dressing. They also both reported that they became popular within weeks throughout the city, where they were (and are still) simply called 'wings' or 'chicken wings'.

As well-known as (both versions) of the Bellissimo family tale are, many other Buffalonians have made it clear that they believe they invented the chicken wing, or know someone who 'really did' invent the chicken wing.

One of the better-known claimants is a man named John Young, who once owned a restaurant named John Young's Wings 'n' Things in Buffalo during the mid-1960s. Mr Young served his wings breaded and whole, though, and featured a special 'mambo sauce'.

While it's uncertain which big-bang theory of the chicken wing is most accurate, what happened over the next few decades is clear: buffalo chicken wings exploded in popularity across the country. During the 1970s, the recipe spread to other eateries in the city and state, and many restaurants in Buffalo learned quickly how

to make their version delicious. Duff's was one such establishment, and it is now a favourite wing joint of many Buffalonians.

Nowadays, buffalo sauce has gone beyond wings – it's frequently used for boneless chicken fingers, pizzas and sandwich wraps. We put Buffalo sauce on burgers, on sandwiches, and petrol/gas stations sell everything from buffalo-flavoured crisps/potato chips to buffalo-flavoured beef jerky.

Those of us who don't have a connection to Buffalo are just as savvy. We fry them, coat them in sauce and serve them at every corner in the U.S. If there is a bar with a menu, you will most likely find a regional version of Buffalo chicken wings.

In Buffalo, though, wings are still eaten roughly the way they were invented by Teressa in 1964: served in either hot, medium or mild buffalo sauce, with blue cheese and celery.

In 1977, the city of Buffalo proclaimed 29th July to be 'Chicken Wing Day'. The city also hosts the annual National Chicken Wing Festival on the Monday of the Labor Day weekend (occurring on the first Monday of September), which now attracts around 90,000 visitors a year. It also includes the US Chicken Wing Eating Championship, which attracts quite a crowd!

Suppliers & Stockists

Poultry

TJ's Free Range Poultry
T: 815-686-9200

W: www.GreenCityMarket.Org/Farmers

Chickens and turkeys have the run of fenced pastures at Timothy and Julie Ifft's central Illinois farm. The couple's feathered friends are fed an all-natural diet of corn and soybean meal, with no hormones or animal by-products.

Honey Hill Farm
T: 585-346-3829

W: http://honeyhillorganicfarm.com/real-chicken

Certified organic, pasture-raised birds raised in upstate New York. Honey Hill Farm chickens live their lives on clean, fresh grass, eating only organically-raised grains and pasture grasses. They are treated humanely and kindly.

Condiments

Golden State Pickle Works
https://www.etsy.com/uk/shop/GSPickleWorks

The Golden State Pickle Works stocks the modern food lovers' larder. Using the bounty of northern California's Sonoma County to make artisanal fermented vegetables, fruit and thoughtfully crafted condiments, from hot sauce to apricot ketchup and artisanal mustards. They carry on the traditions of the American food pantry while also contributing to the dialogue. By supporting local farmers and their beautiful produce, they practise one of the oldest and purest forms of preservation to be enjoyed throughout the year.

Mouth
W: http://www.mouth.com/collections/condiments

Most of the products on this site are made by small, independent producers in New York, but you'll also find a few unique non-New York indie food items.

Sauce Suppliers

Frank's RedHot
T: 1-800-841-1256

www.franksredhot.com

Frank's RedHot hot sauce was established in Springfield, Missouri in 1920. It also holds the illustrious title of being the main ingredient in the first buffalo wing sauce created in 1964 at the Anchor Bar and Grill in Buffalo.

Louisiana Hot Sauce Original
T: 1-800-299-9082

W: www.louisianapepper.com

They claim to be one of 'the very first commercially available Cajun food products' and the 'first hot sauce to use the state's name'. Established in 1928, they are one of the most commercially used hot sauces by a variety of wing-based restaurant establishments.

Dr Burnorium's Hot Sauce Emporium (UK)

Exchange Hall

Corn Street

Bristol

BS1 1JQ

T: +44 01179-300-175

W: http://www.hotsauceemporium.co.uk

A large array of hot chilli sauces, chilli extracts, BBQ sauces, hot mustards, wing sauces, chilli seasonings, chilli rubs and fiery snacks.

Fryers and Grill Supplies

Fry Daddy Electric Deep Fryer

T: 1-800-877-0401

W: www.gopresto.com

Presto's Fry Daddy fryers are ideal because they use a limited amount of oil and they keep temperatures consistent.

King Kooker

T: 1-800-732-0601

W: www.kingkooker.com

King Kooker's online store offers a variety of grilling products, from chicken wing racks, that help wings cook more evenly on a grill, almost smoking them, to deep fryers and smokers.

CHICKEN WING FESTIVALS

The National Buffalo Chicken Wings Festival

T: 716-565-4141

W: www.buffalowing.com

Founded in 2002 by 'Wing King' Drew Cerza, the National Buffalo Wing Festival is a weekend festival held at Coca-Cola Field in downtown Buffalo, New York, USA, celebrating the Buffalo-style chicken wing. The festival is held on Labor Day weekend and culminates with the IFOCE sanctioned Buffalo Wing eating contest.

Southern Hot Wing Festival

W: www.southernhotwingfestival.com

Established in 2003 by a local Memphain who felt that the South had more to offer than just amazingly great BBQ, the Southern Hot Wing festival has become a staple event each April. Boasting, on average, around 50+ teams a year, the Southern Hot Wing festival glorifies the almighty chicken (wing) in much the same way that Memphis BBQ has done with the pig.

London Wing Fest (UK)

W: www.wingfest.co.uk

A celebration of the magnificent chicken wing! Inspired by the annual Buffalo Wing Festival in New York State where 2.4 million chicken wings are consumed over two days, London Wing Fest is the creation of two huge wing fans, Richard and Andy, who run a chicken wing restaurant in London called Randy's Wing Bar.

Index